Hazana

Hazana

Jewish Vegetarian Cooking

PAOLA GAVIN

PHOTOGRAPHY BY MOWIE KAY

ILLUSTRATIONS BY LIZ CATCHPOLE

quadrille

To Alfred and Tilly

'He who has fed a stranger,
may have fed an angel.'

The Talmud

Over their two thousand years of exile, Jews migrated
across the world, taking their culinary heritage and
traditions with them. Wherever they went, they
adapted local and regional dishes to fit their own
strict dietary laws and, as a result, Jewish food today
encompasses an enormous variety of cuisines and
cooking styles. This book is a personal collection of
traditional Jewish vegetarian dishes from around the
world. The recipes I have chosen have been passed
on from mother to daughter for generations, and are
quick, easy to prepare and healthy.

The Jewish concept of vegetarianism dates back to the days of the Garden of Eden. Under traditional Jewish law it was forbidden to kill an animal, just as it was to kill a man. In Judaism, as in Hinduism, the eating of meat is thought to increase the animal nature of man, and Jews are forbidden to eat any meat 'in which its lifeblood still runs' as this is thought to contain the spirit, emotions and instinct of the animal.

The diet of the ancient nomadic Israelites was predominantly vegetarian. Sheep, goats and cattle were too highly prized for their milk production to be killed for their flesh, so livestock was mainly slaughtered for ritual practices. When the Hebrews fled to Egypt, they adopted new eating habits: Egyptians taught them the art of making leavened bread, and they soon shared the Egyptian love of cucumbers, melons, leeks, onions and garlic.

After the Jews arrived in the Holy Land they became farmers, growing wheat, barley, rye and millet. The food of the poor was based on bread, pulses – especially lentils, broad (fava) beans and lupins - goat's and sheep's cheese, olives and olive oil, nuts, vegetables and herbs, and fresh and dried fruit. Food was usually sweetened with honey or syrup made from figs, carob beans or dates; at that time, Jericho was famous for its dates and was nicknamed 'the city of palm trees'.

One ancient Jewish sect – the Essenes – were staunch vegetarians. The mostly male sect existed in the second century BC. It was formed in reaction to the rigidity of Jewish religion of that time. The word Essene derives from the Hebrew word *esau*, meaning 'to be strong', and presumably this referred to their strength of mind, the renunciation of material comforts and repression of sexual desire. John the Baptist is said to have been an Essene, and there are some people who believe that Jesus spent some of his early years with the Essene community.

There are four main Jewish communities across the world: the Mizachrim, or Easterners, whose ancestry is from the Middle and Near East, Afghanistan, Uzbekistan and India; the Ashkenazim, who settled in the Rhineland after the diaspora and then migrated across Eastern Europe to Russia and the Ukraine; the Sephardim, or Spanish Jews, who settled around the Mediterranean after fleeing the Spanish Inquisition; and the Italkim, Italian Jews who were brought to Italy as slaves by the Roman Emperor Titus, following the destruction of the Second Temple.

Nevertheless, close trading and cultural connections mean that these cuisines often have similarities. For example, there are strong ties between the Jews of Tunisia and those of Livorno in Italy – which is reflected in their cooking. The Italian *cuscussu* is obviously of North African origin, while the Tunisian *boka di dama* (almond sponge cake) clearly has Italian roots.

Ultimately, Jewish cooking is food cooked according to the Kashrut (Jewish dietary laws), that forbid the consumption of meat and milk at the same meal. In Orthodox Jewish households, separate plates, utensils, pots and pans are used for milk and meat. Milk products cannot be eaten after meat until an interval of time has lapsed. This can vary from 2 to 6 hours according to local tradition. Neutral food, such as milk-based bread, fruit, vegetables and unfertilized eggs can be consumed with meat or milk.

Researching this book has been a great opportunity to discover the history and culinary heritage not only of my own family – who originally came from Poland and Belarus – but also to trace the history and culinary traditions of Jews from so many different parts of the world. One thing we all have in common is the same love of food and cooking, something that lies at the heart of Jewish life.

Jewish holidays and festivals

Shabbat

The Sabbath is a weekly day of rest, beginning on Friday just before sundown and ending just after dark on Saturday, when the first three stars can be seen in the sky. During the Sabbath all work is forbidden. 'Work' covers thirty-nine actions, ranging from the lighting of a fire, cooking and baking, to the answering of the telephone. The Sabbath is always ushered in by the lighting of candles, before blessings are said, first over wine and then over a *challah* (braided egg-enriched bread) that is traditionally covered with a white cloth.

Sabbath meals need to be prepared, or at least partly cooked, before sunset on Friday, and ingenious ways were found to accommodate this. One-pot meals and stews that were cooked very slowly overnight were invented, such as the Sephardic *dafina* and Ashkenazi *cholent*. Other well-known Sabbath dishes include the Ashkenazi *borscht* (beetroot soup), *krupnik* (mushroom and barley soup) and *kugels* (sweet or savoury puddings); and the Sephardic *huevos haminados* (slow-baked eggs) and *borekas*, *bulemas*, *pastels* and *filas* (cheese or vegetable pastries). Italian Jews often prepare stuffed vegetables, caponata or minestrone soup for the Sabbath.

Rosh Hashanah

Rosh Hashanah falls around the end of September or early October (on the first two days of the Hebrew month of Tishri), and marks the beginning of the Ten Days of Repentance, which end with the Day of Atonement (Yom Kippur). Jews believe there is a Book of Life in heaven, in which all our thoughts, words and deeds are recorded. During the Days of Repentance, this book is examined and everyone's fate for the coming year is decided.

Traditional foods served for Rosh Hashanah are black-eyed beans (peas), leeks, beet greens, gourds and dates. It is customary to eat *challah* or a slice of apple dipped in honey, and to say a prayer for a sweet New Year. Sometimes pomegranates are served, as their plentiful seeds symbolize good deeds for the year ahead. Ashkenazis also like to serve carrot *tsimmes* (a sweet stew) as a symbol of good luck, *kugels*, *lekach* (honey cake) and *teiglach* (pastry nuggets cooked in honey). Sephardic Jews prefer rice pilafs, *almodrote* (gratins) and pastries soaked in sugar syrup. Nothing sharp or bitter is served for New Year, nor anything black, because of its association with mourning.

Yom Kippur

Sukkot

Yom Kippur is the most solemn and holy day of the year, a day of fasting and reflection. The last meal before the fast is served in the late afternoon of the eve of Yom Kippur, and it never includes salty food, as it is not easy to fast when you are thirsty. In Egypt this meal often begins with an egg and lemon soup. Ashkenazis often prepare a broth with *kneidlach* (matzo balls) or *kreplach* (a kind of ravioli). In the Sephardic world, the fast is usually broken with a cold drink based on almonds, melon seeds, sour cherries or grenadine (a syrup made from pomegranates), followed by a light dairy meal that might include *borekas* or *sambusak* (spinach and cheese turnovers). Ashkenazis enjoy *teiglach* and fruit strudels. Sephardic Jews prefer rice pilafs, gratins (*almodrote*) and pastries soaked in honey, especially *tishpishti*, *travados*, *sansathicos* and baklava. Syrian Jews like to break the fast with little courgette (zucchini) and white cheese omelettes, tomato salad, olives and fresh fruit.

Sukkot starts five days after Yom Kippur and lasts for seven or eight days. The *sukkah* – meaning 'booth' – represents the huts the Jews lived in during their forty years of wandering in the desert after their Exodus from Egypt. To celebrate the festival, temporary huts are constructed outdoors and decorated with the branches of four symbolic plants: citron, willow, palm and myrtle. The roofs are made of separated fronds, so you can see the stars, and meals are usually eaten in the huts throughout the festival.

Simchat Torah – literally 'the joy of the Torah' – is the last day of Sukkot, when the annual reading of the five Books of Moses comes to an end. Sukkot is also known as the Harvest Festival and meals always include a wide variety of vegetables and fruits, as well as sweets and pastries made with nuts, apples, quinces, pumpkins or grapes. Stuffed cabbage or cabbage strudel are often prepared by Ashkenazi Jews, while Italian Jews make a variety of vegetable soups and gratins. Sephardic communities in Morocco usually make couscous with vegetables or bean soups.

Chanukah

Chanukah falls around the middle of December (on the twenty-fifth day of the Hebrew month of Kisler) and lasts for eight days. A celebration of freedom and bravery, Chanukah commemorates the re-dedication of the Temple of Jerusalem after the victorious uprising of Judah Maccabee against the Syrian Hellenists in 165 BC. When Judah entered the desecrated temple, he discovered just enough holy oil to light the menorah for one day, but miraculously the oil lasted for eight whole days until a fresh supply could be found. Ever since, Chanukah has been celebrated by lighting candles in the home, beginning with one candle and adding another each night until eight candles are lit. Fried food, such as Ashkenazi *latkes* (potato pancakes) or Sephardic *fritikas* (sweet or savoury fritters), are associated with Chanukah because of the miracle of the oil. The Sephardim of North Africa often make *chakchouka* (a dish of fried vegetables with eggs) and *sfenj, zalabia* and *yoyos* (sweet fried pastries fritters soaked in sugar syrup).

Tu Bi-Shevat

The minor festival of Tu Bi-Shevat falls around the end of January or early February (on the fifteenth day of the Hebrew month of Shevat), when the first buds appear on the trees in Israel. Sephardic Jews sometimes call it *las Fruticas*, the Festival of Fruits, as all kinds of fresh and dried fruit and nuts are eaten during the celebrations. Some families serve up to thirty different kinds of fruit. Traditionally, four glasses of wine are served with the evening meal: the first is white wine; the second contains white wine mixed with a little red wine; the third consists of red and white wine in equal quantities; and the fourth is red wine mixed with a little white. Each glass is accompanied by some bread, with fruit or nuts served in the following order: olive, date, grape, fig, pomegranate, lemon, apple, walnut, almond, carob and pear.

Purim

Pesach

Purim falls around the middle of March (on the fourteenth day of the Hebrew month of Adar) and lasts for two days. It commemorates the way Queen Ester of Persia outwitted the king's advisor, Haman, who had decreed the killing of all Jews. Purim is traditionally celebrated with street parades, pageants and little improvised plays. Purim is the only festival in the Jewish year when it is a commandment, or mitzvah, to get drunk. Purim is always celebrated with a vegetarian meal because Queen Ester was vegetarian while she lived in her Persian palace, as the kitchen was not kosher. Iranian Jews usually prepare a *kuku* (omelette) or *shirin polo* (sweet rice), while Algerian Jews serve *couscous au beurre* (couscous with butter and broad (fava) beans). Traditionally all kinds of sweet pastries are made, especially the Ashkenazi *hamantaschen* (literally, 'Haman's pockets') - triangular pastries filled with poppy seeds, raisins or prune jam; and the Sephardic *diblas* or *orejas de Haman* (literally, 'Haman's ears'), nut-filled pastries in sugar syrup. Italian Jews often make cheese or spinach ravioli, and sweet or savoury turnovers called *buricche*.

Passover begins in March or April (on the fourteenth day of the Hebrew month of Nisan) and lasts for seven or eight days. It celebrates the liberation of the Jews from slavery in Egypt. To mark the fact that the Jews left in such haste that their bread had no time to rise, it is forbidden to eat any leavened foods (*hametz*) or fermenting agents like yeast, or grains that can be fermented, such as wheat, rye, barley, oats and spelt. Homes are always spring-cleaned in preparation for Passover and all cooking utensils, cutlery and dishes are packed away and replaced by a fresh set that is reserved exclusively for this holiday.

Special foods are made for the ritual meal, or Seder, that takes place on the first two nights of Passover: roasted or boiled eggs are served as a symbol of sacrifice and rebirth; and *maror* (bitter herbs) dipped in salt or vinegar symbolize the bitterness of slavery. *Haroset* (a dried fruit and nut paste) represents the mortar the Jews used for building when they were slaves in Egypt, and of course matzo is a reminder that there was no time for the bread to rise before they made good their escape.

The strict dietary restrictions that apply during Passover have produced an enormous variety of dishes made with matzo meal, potato flour and rice flour. The Jews of Turkey make delicious baked omelettes or gratins with potatoes, leeks, eggplants (aubergines), courgettes (zucchini), Swiss chard or pumpkin. All kinds of desserts and cakes are made with ground almonds, walnuts or hazelnuts, such as Eastern European *chremslach* or *bubeleh* (matzo-meal pancakes), Italian *scodelline* (rich almond custards), German and Austrian *nusstorten* (nut cakes), and *koopeta* (nut candy) from Greece.

THE FESTIVAL OF WEEKS

Shavuot

Shavuot falls at the end of May or beginning of June (on the sixth day of the Hebrew month of Sivan), fifty days or seven weeks after Passover (Shavuot means 'weeks'), and it coincides with Pentecost, meaning 'fiftieth' in Greek. It marks the time when Moses received the Ten Commandments on Mount Sinai, and is also a harvest festival, celebrating the ripening of the first fruit on the trees in Israel. Traditionally a dairy meal is served, followed by plenty of fresh fruit. White foods, such as rice or white cornmeal, are often eaten as they symbolize purity. Foods prepared for Shavuot include the Ashkenazi cheese *blintzes* (filled pancakes); Syrian cheese *sambusak* (turnovers) and *kalsonnes* (ravioli); Sephardic *borekas*, *boyos* or *filas* (savoury pastries); and Algerian *couscous au beurre* (couscous with butter and broad [fava] beans).

Tisha Be-Av

The minor festival of Tisha Be-Av falls around the middle of July or early August (on the ninth day of the Hebrew month of Av); it commemorates the destruction of the First Temple in Jerusalem in 586 BC, and of the Second Temple in 70 AD. The three weeks before Tisha Be-Av are a period of mourning - often called the *schwarzen wochen* ('black weeks') by Ashkenazi Jews – when no weddings or other festivities are celebrated, and no new items of clothing may be worn. During this period, observant Jews also abstain from eating meat or drinking wine, except on the Sabbath. Vegetarian or dairy meals are prepared, especially dishes with lentils – traditionally associated with grief – such as Moroccan *harira* (lentil and rice soup), Syrian *mujaddara* (lentils and rice with caramelized onions) and Greek *lentejas a la djiudia* (green lentils simmered with onions and tomatoes).

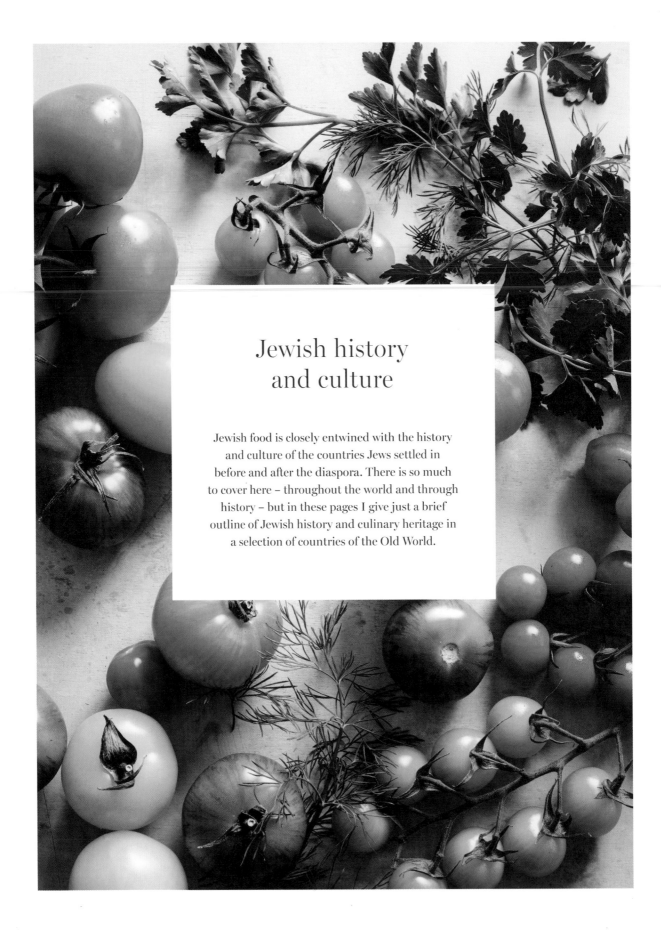

Jewish history and culture

Jewish food is closely entwined with the history and culture of the countries Jews settled in before and after the diaspora. There is so much to cover here – throughout the world and through history – but in these pages I give just a brief outline of Jewish history and culinary heritage in a selection of countries of the Old World.

Austria

Jews have lived in Austria for the best part of a thousand years. In the thirteenth and fourteenth centuries, Vienna had one of the largest and most important Jewish communities in Europe, until they suffered a series of persecutions and expulsions that lasted more than 200 years.

Nevertheless, by the end of the seventeenth century, a small number of wealthy financiers and merchants rose to prominence and were given special status as *hofjuden* ('court Jews'), who helped finance the court and the army. Some Jewish families even had their own coat of arms.

Gradually, as the spirit of the Enlightenment spread through Europe, life began to improve for the whole community. In 1781, the Holy Roman Emperor Joseph II issued an Edict of Toleration, which gave the Jews access to trade and industry. They were no longer required to wear badges or special hats, and their children could attend state schools and universities. They were, however, forced to adopt German names, and the use of Yiddish and Hebrew were restricted, in a vain attempt to assimilate them.

It was not until the mid-nineteenth century that Jews were finally granted full equal rights. For some it was a time of great upheaval and confusion, as they left their small towns and villages in search of new opportunities in the cities. Although many were poor and working class, a large number of Jews went into business, the transport industry, the liberal professions and the arts. By the turn of the century, Vienna had become a magnet for Jewish cultural and intellectual life – home to Arnold Schonberg, Gustav Mahler, Stefan Zweig, Theodore Herzl (founder of Zionism), Sigmund Freud and Oscar Kokoschka, to name a few. A large number of the city's bankers, doctors and lawyers were Jewish, as were many publishers, journalists and most of the Austrian Socialist Party. At the same time, anti-Semitism was widespread, and in the inter-war period the situation rapidly deteriorated; so much so that many thousands of Jews left the country before 1938.

Austrian Jewish cooking is classic Ashkenazi fare, with lots of substantial soups, often served with noodles (*nudeln*), fried pasta puffs (*mandeln*) or dumplings (*knodeln*). There is a liking for potatoes, cabbage and sauerkraut. All kinds of sweet and savoury soufflés and pancakes (*palatchinken*) are made, as well as pasta dishes, such as noodles with curd cheese (*nudeln mit topfen*) or with poppy seeds (*mohnnudeln*). Fruit puddings and compotes are often served for the Sabbath. Vienna, of course, is famous for its superb cakes, pastries, strudels and tortes – layered cakes, usually eaten in the middle of the day with a cup of coffee or hot chocolate. Hazelnut sponge cake (*nusstorte*) and ginger cookies (*ingerlakh*) are often served for Passover.

Czech and Slovak republics

Jews first came to the Czech Republic at the time of the first
Crusade, fleeing persecution in the Rhineland. Most settled in
Prague, where they were restricted to earning a living by money-
lending or selling second-hand clothing.

In the second half of the thirteenth century, they
were moved into a Judenstadt (Jewish quarter),
and shortly after King Ottaker II granted them
religious and civil autonomy.

In the centuries that followed, the Jewish
community endured persecution and expulsions,
but a small number were allowed to remain, as
long as they paid special taxes, wore distinctive
badges, and complied with trade and business
restrictions. By the late sixteenth century, some
Jews had risen to positions of great importance:
Emperor Rudolf II had a Jewish finance
minister, Mordechai Maisel, who became one
of the richest men in Bohemia. Maisel not only
bought the Jewish quarter, but also financed
the building of the town hall, a bath-house and
several synagogues. At the time, Prague had the
largest and most important Jewish community
in Europe.

However, Jews were not granted equal rights
until after the fall of the Austro-Hungarian
Empire at the end of World War I. In 1935 the
Jewish community of Prague numbered more
than 350,000, but after World War II many
of the surviving Jews emigrated to Israel and
America, and by 1947 only 8,000 remained.

The first major Jewish settlement in Slovakia
was in the sixteenth century, in Pressburg (now
called Bratislava), but it was several hundred
years before the city became an important centre
of Jewish education. A *yeshivah* (religious
teaching institution) was set up in 1808 that was
to become one of the most important Orthodox
establishments in Europe. By the 1930s
Bratislava had nineteen synagogues and almost
ten per cent of the population was Jewish, but
only a few thousand Jews survived the war.

The Jewish cooking of the Czech and Slovak
republics is classic Ashkenazi cooking: beetroot
(beet), potato and cucumber salads; sweet and
savoury dumplings (*galushkas*, *halusky* or
knedliky); warming vegetable soups, especially
beetroot (*borsc*) and potato (*bramborova
polevka*); fruit compotes, and a wide variety
of fruit cakes, strudels, pancakes (*palacinky*)
and doughnuts. Both Czechs and Slovaks love
potatoes, which are made into dumplings,
puddings, fritters, pancakes (*latkes* or *preklech*),
omelettes and rissoles, or simply served boiled
or baked with sour cream or goat's cheese. All
kinds of delicious cakes and pastries are made,
including chocolate almond cake (*caruso*); sweet
pastries called *hamantaschen* filled with
plum povidl (prune jam); and sponge cake
topped with cherries (*bublanina*).

Egypt

There have been Jewish communities in Egypt since ancient times:
after the destruction of the First Temple in 586 BC many Jews
settled in Alexandria and the Nile Valley, and by the first century
AD there were over a million Jews in Egypt.

Following the Arab conquest in the eighth century, the Jews – considered 'People of the Book' – were better treated by the Muslims than they had been by the Christian Romans. Nevertheless, they were still forced to live in ghettos, pay a punitive poll tax, and endure many other restrictions. At this time, most Jews were merchants, craftsmen, artisans, silversmiths, goldsmiths, street traders and money-changers.

The expulsion of Jews from Spain and Portugal in the sixteenth century brought a wave of refugees to Alexandria. Welcomed for their much-needed skills and expertise, they came to be known as the Espagnoli. The nineteenth century brought another influx of Jewish immigrants to Egypt from Syria, Greece, Turkey and the Balkans, especially after the opening of the Suez Canal in 1869 and the advent of British colonial rule in 1882. The cosmopolitan cities of Alexandria and Cairo, and the rapidly expanding economy, also attracted European Jews, mainly well-educated professionals, wealthy merchants and financiers, who were dubbed *haute Juiverie*,

as they moved in the upper echelons of Egyptian society. However, most Jews left the country after the Suez Crisis in 1956.

Egyptian Jewish cooking reflects the cultural mix of the Jewish community, with many Sephardic dishes from the Balkans and Syria. The cuisine is based on fresh fruit and vegetables, nuts and seeds, pulses and grains – especially rice and bulgur – and a small amount of dairy products. There is a liking for stuffed vegetables (*dolma*) and thick frittata-like omelettes called *eggah*, while the dish of lentils, rice and macaroni known as *koshary* is enjoyed by Egyptians and Jews alike. Sabbath dishes include stewed broad (fava) beans (*ful medames*), served with boiled eggs simmered overnight with onion skins (*beid hamine*), and savoury pastries, usually filled with cheese or spinach (*sambusak, filas* and *borekitas*). Sweet nut-filled pastries in syrup – especially baklava and konafa – are traditionally prepared for births, circumcisions and other festive occasions; and a sweet bread called *masmousa* is generally served to break the fast of Yom Kippur.

France

There have been Jewish settlements in France since the days
of the Roman Empire, when most Jews lived around Masillia
(Marseilles), with smaller communities in Tolosa (Toulouse),
Burdigalia (Bordeaux) and the north.

Under the reign of Charlemagne, in the eighth
century, many Jews settled in the Rhone Valley
and Champagne, which was then famous for
its trade fairs. At that time, most Jews were
merchants, traders, vintners, cheese-makers
and bakers. However, the Crusades brought
with them increasing persecution, and many
Jews fled to Alsace-Lorraine, then part of
the German Holy Roman Empire. In 1394
all Jews were forced to leave the country,
except for those in the southern enclaves of
Avignon and the Comtat Venaissin, which were
under Papal rule. These communities were
Ashkenazi, but after the Spanish Inquisition
in 1492 many Sephardim settled in Bordeaux,
Bayonne and Nantes in the west, and in
Toulouse, Montpellier and Marseilles to the
south. However, the majority of Jews still lived
in Alsace and Lorraine, which became part of
France in the seventeenth century. After the
French Revolution in 1791, Jews were granted
full equality under Napoleon's Declaration of the
Rights of Man.

In the early twentieth century another wave of
Jewish immigrants arrived, mainly from Eastern
Europe, soon outnumbering the old Jewish
communities of Alsace and Lorraine. They were
followed in the 1960s by an influx of North
African Jews from the former French territories
of Morocco, Algeria and Tunisia, who make up
the majority of Jews in France today.

The influence of Jewish cooking on the food
of Alsace and Lorraine is reflected in the many
local dishes prepared *à la juive* ('in the Jewish
style'). There is also a strong German influence,
with a liking for noodles (*frimsels*) and
dumplings, especially potato dumplings served
with melted butter and grated cheese (*knepfle*).
The most popular vegetables are potatoes and
cabbage, which are often cooked *ziss-sauer*
in the Jewish way – with sugar, cinnamon
and vinegar. Rice with prunes and raisins
(*reizfloimes*) is often served for the Sabbath, as
is a deep-dish apple pie called *apfel shalet* or
chalet à la juive. Delicious pastries are prepared,
especially creamy onion or cheese quiches, and
fruit tarts made with cherries, apples, apricots
and mirabelle plums.

The Jews of Morocco, Algeria and Tunisia have
also had an impact on modern French cooking:
in the Jewish areas of Paris and Marseilles, you
will find many North African restaurants and
food stores serving couscous, exotic *tajines* or
stews, and numerous sweet pastries filled with
almond paste and soaked in syrup.

Germany

During the eighth-century reign of Charlemagne a large number
of Jews settled in Germany, especially in small towns and villages
along the Rhine. Because of their strict dietary laws, many of them
went into the food trade.

Some became bakers and farmers, raising diary cows and poultry, especially geese; others made cheese or sold pickles and preserves; and a few produced their own wine.

By the time of the Crusades, many Jews had also become traders, importing sugar, spices, nuts and dried fruit from the Orient, and craftsmen, working as spinners, weavers and jewellers. But the Crusades brought persecution and restrictions: Jews were no longer allowed to own land, and many lost the right to trade and so had to resort to earning a living as peddlers in second-hand clothing or becoming money-lenders. With the arrival of the Black Death in 1349, many fell into poverty and fled to Poland and Eastern Europe.

By the end of the sixteenth century, many of the Jews who remained were forced into ghettos called *Judengasse* ('Jewish quarters'), each with their own synagogue, slaughterhouse, cemetery, communal baths, bakery and a *tanzhaus* (literally 'dance hall') that was also used for weddings and special occasions.

In the seventeenth century, when much of the German Empire was divided into principalities, many Jews rose to prominence as court Jews, since the rulers of most of these territories employed a Jewish auxiliary to administer their finances, equip the army and furnish their court with precious stones and textiles. For the majority of the Jewish population, however, things did not improve until the eighteenth century, when industrialization brought new opportunities for them to use their business acumen – and some families, notably the Rothschilds, accumulated great wealth. In 1871 Jews were emancipated from the ghettoes, and many subsequently became renowned in intellectual, scientific and artistic circles. Nevertheless, a new wave of anti-Semitism in the 1880s prompted thousands to emigrate to America.

German Jewish cooking is heavy and substantial, replete with sweet and savoury puddings and warming soups – often made from lentils, split peas or beans, and served with dumplings, noodles or fried pasta puffs. The predominant vegetables are beetroots (beets), cabbage and especially potatoes, which are made into potato puddings (*kartoffel kugeln*), potato pancakes (*latkes*) and potato puffs (*bilkas*). Cucumbers are often made into dill pickles. Traditional cakes and pastries include honey cake (*lekach*) for Rosh Hashanah; twice-baked almond bread (*mandelbrot*), sweet pastries filled with poppy seeds (*hamantaschen*), and spicy pepper biscuits (*pfeffernuesse*) for Purim. Plum cake (*pflaumenkuchen*) is traditionally served to break the Fast of Yom Kippur.

Hungary

Jews first came to Hungary in Roman times when the land was part of the province of Pannonia. They were followed by Khazar Jews from the Caucasus, who arrived in the tenth century, and many Ashkenazi Jews from Germany and Czechoslovakia during the Middle Ages.

By the end of the thirteenth century, there was a Jewish quarter in Buda, with its own synagogue – and a cemetery outside the city walls.

In the sixteenth century, much of present-day Hungary came under Ottoman Turkish rule, and Jews were granted more freedoms, including the right to trade, especially with other regions of the Ottoman Empire. Turkish rule lasted until 1668, when the Austrians recaptured Buda, decimating the Jewish community for its loyalty to the Ottoman Turks. The majority of the surviving Jews lived on landowner estates in the country, or in the market town of Obuda (literally 'old Buda'), just outside the capital. At this time most Jews were shopkeepers or traders in sugar cane, scrap iron, sheep or hare skins, or were involved in the textile industry. Following the Holy Roman Emperor Joseph II's Edict of Toleration in 1782, some Jews moved back to the city, but they were not granted full emancipation until 1868. By 1930 more than a quarter of the population of Budapest was Jewish. Although many Jews lost their lives during the Holocaust, there is still a thriving Jewish community in the city.

Hungarian Jewish cooking is a mix of Central European and Sephardic cuisines. There are many vegetable soups (*leves*), often enriched with sour cream or served with a variety of dumplings (*gomboc*, *shliskes* and *galuskas*). There is a fondness for cauliflower, potatoes, mushrooms, cabbage, and especially sweet (bell) peppers – either stuffed with rice and tomatoes or made into *lecso*, a dish of stewed peppers and tomatoes richly flavoured with paprika. Noodles (*metelt*) may be served with curd cheese, or sweetened with sugar or honey and topped with ground walnuts or poppy seeds.

All kinds of strudels (*retes*) are made with apple, sour cherry, plum, poppy seed, almond, curd cheese or even cabbage. A pastry layered with chopped nuts, apple and poppy seeds (*flodni*) and rolled cookies filled with chopped walnuts, raisins and honey (*knidli*) are traditionally served for Purim. *Teiglach* (pellets of dough cooked in honey with ginger and nutmeg) are usually made to celebrate Rosh Hashanah.

Iran (Persia)

The Persian Jewish community dates back to the 539 BC, when Cyrus the Great conquered Babylon. By the third century AD, Jewish communities had sprung up across the Persian Empire in Susa, Isfahan, Shiraz and Hamadan, and as far away as Bukhara and Samarkand.

For more than a thousand years, Jewish merchants travelled and settled along the old silk and spice routes that linked the Middle East with India and China.

Jews fared well under Sunni Muslim rule. Considered 'People of the Book', they were free to practise their religious traditions as long as they paid the *jeziyeh* – a special poll tax imposed on non-Muslim minorities, giving them the right to pursue their faith.

But the Shiite Safavid era in the sixteenth century brought social and economic change; there were persecutions and some Jewish communities were forced to convert – or be expelled. Most Jews eked out a living as money-lenders, artisans, merchants or traders in second-hand goods, while others made and sold herbal medicine, or pursued cultural and artistic endeavours: several well-known Jewish poets were working in Persia during this period, and some fine Judeo-Persian manuscripts were produced. During this time, Jews were not permitted to have a shop in the bazaar or city streets, use public baths or drink from a public well, and so most of them chose to live in a muhalleh (Jewish quarter), where they had their own markets, bakeries and baths.

By the nineteenth century, there were 30,000 Jews living in Iran. Some were bankers, treasurers or court officials, but most were small businessmen dealing in textiles, antiques, jewellery or spices. There were also a number of Jewish musicians, minstrels and dancers. After the Constitutional Revolution of 1906, Jews were no longer required to pay the *jeziyeh* and some left the *muhallehs*. Nevertheless, in 1948 more than 40,000 Jews emigrated to the newly formed state of Israel.

Persian cooking has a large repertoire of vegetarian dishes, as traditionally Persians only eat small amounts of meat. In summertime a family meal may simply consist of wholemeal (whole wheat) naan bread, some white goat or cow's milk cheese similar to feta, a bowl of fresh herbs, and perhaps a yoghurt and vegetable dish called a *boorani*, followed by fresh fruit for dessert. Warming vegetable soups such as kidney bean, spinach and noodle soup (*ash-e-reshteh*) or a vegetable omelette (*kuku*) are popular in winter. Dried limes and pomegranate syrup are widely used for flavouring. There is also a fondness for stuffed vegetables (*dolmeh*), and rice pilaf (*polow*) made with spinach, herbs, carrots, broad (fava) beans, lentils, sour cherries, nuts or dried fruit. Sweet saffron rice with carrots, almonds, pistachios and dried orange peel (*shireen polow*) is traditionally served for weddings and special occasions.

Iraq

There have been Jewish communities in Iraq since biblical times.
After King Nebuchadnezzar captured Jerusalem and destroyed the
First Temple in 586 BC, the Jews were exiled to Babylon, not far
from present-day Baghdad.

At that time, Babylonia had one of the most developed cultures in the world, and the Babylonians introduced the Jews to new methods of market gardening and fruit growing, as well as to rice and exotic spices such as ginger.

Within fifty years, Babylon was overrun by King Cyrus of Persia and, although he granted permission for Jews to return to their homeland, many chose to stay. New synagogues and academies for studying Jewish Law were established, and by the third century AD Baghdad had overtaken Palestine as the centre of World Jewry. Jews flourished for the next 700 years, under Greek, Roman and Arab rule; most were involved in agriculture and trade, especially in precious stones, spices and silks from China.

Over the following centuries, the fortunes of the Jewish community fluctuated. When Tamerlane advanced on Baghdad in 1393, many Jews fled to Syria and Kurdistan. Then, in the late eighteenth century, a number of Jews emigrated to Persia and India, mainly to escape persecution, but also to seek out new markets and business opportunities in the East.

Nevertheless, when Iraq became a British mandate at the end of World War I, over a third of the population of Baghdad was Jewish.

In 1921, Faisal I was put in place as king, and the Jews of Baghdad were granted 'freedom of religion, education and employment'. However, after the state of Israel was formed in 1948, the Jews were again subject to persecution, and in 1951 most Iraqi Jews were airlifted to Israel in a mass exodus known as Operation Ezra and Nehemiah.

The cuisine of Iraqi Jews is greatly influenced by the Persians and the Ottoman Turks. From the Persians they adopted a taste for sweet and sour dishes made with vinegar, tamarind or pomegranate molasses, and fruit in savoury dishes. The Ottoman Turks introduced them to rice dishes, stuffed vegetables (*mahasha*), and a variety of sweet and savoury pastries, such as the cheese-filled *sambusak*, and others filled with spinach or chickpeas. There is a liking for stewed chickpeas (*lablabi*), okra stew (*bamia*), and a dish of sweet and sour pumpkin simmered with raisins, almonds and dried apricots (*tershana*) that is traditionally prepared for Tu Bi-Shevat. Other festival foods include fried pastries soaked in sugar syrup (*zlabiya*) made for Chanukah, and sweet yeasted pancakes called *kahi* that are usually served for breakfast on the morning after Passover.

Italy

Jews have lived in Italy for more than 2,000 years. In fact, Rome
has the oldest Jewish community in western Europe, dating back
to the second century BC.

After Emperor Titus destroyed the Second
Temple in Jerusalem, thousands of Jews were
brought to Rome as slaves, and other Jewish
communities soon sprung up across southern
Italy, in Naples, Calabria, Apulia, Sardinia – and
especially Sicily, which was an important trading
centre for the whole of the Mediterranean.

The Jewish population of Sicily thrived for
more than 1,500 years, under Arab, Norman,
Angevin and Aragonese rule. The Arabs brought
new ingredients: rice, aubergine (eggplant)
and artichokes – and a penchant for sweet and
sour dishes that included raisins and pine nuts.
Arabic influence was so pervasive that some
Jews wore Moorish dress, and many spoke
Arabic and Greek, as well as Italian.

By 1000 AD small Jewish communities had
sprung up all over northern Italy, especially
in Pavia and Lucca, which were important
centres for trade with northern Europe. Most
Jews worked as craftsmen, artisans, traders or
peddlers, but some were peasants and small
landowners, mainly tending olive groves and
vineyards, so they could produce their own wine.

The Jews of these early communities were
known as the Italkim. The Ashkenazim, who
came mainly came from France, Germany and
the Rhineland, did not arrive in Italy until the
thirteenth and fourteenth centuries, at the
time of the Black Death, and they settled

mostly in Piedmont, Venezia-Giulia, Mantua
and Ferrara. The Sephardim came later again,
fleeing the Spanish Inquisition in 1492, and
bringing with them foods from the New World:
tomatoes, potatoes, pumpkins, peppers, beans,
corn and chocolate.

Around the same time, Jews were expelled from
southern Italy, and soon after from the islands
of Sicily and Sardinia, all of which were under
Spanish rule. Most fled to Rome, but many
went north, especially to Pesaro, Ancona and
Venice. The sudden influx of people led to severe
overcrowding in these cities and, as a result,
Jews were segregated in specific quarters and
had to comply with various restrictions. The
first ghetto was created in Venice in 1516, and
by 1556 Pope Paul IV had set up ghettos all over
Italy, where Jews were confined until Napoleon
liberated the ghettos in 1796.

Nevertheless, the Renaissance was a period of
prosperity for many Italian Jews. Some became
bankers and money-lenders (occupations
forbidden to Christians), while others became
merchants, doctors, gem-dealers and scholars.
There were also many Jewish poets, musicians
and composers, who were supported by some of
the greatest arts patrons of the day: the Medicis
of Tuscany, the Viscontis of Milan and the
D'Estes of Ferrara. Others were involved with
the theatre, especially in Mantua, which was
famous for its Jewish actors.

One of the most flourishing centres of Jewish life was Livorno, which was well known for its social, religious and political tolerance, and was the only city in Italy never to have a ghetto. The forward-looking city attracted so many *marranos* (Jews who had openly converted to Christianity, but secretly practiced Judaism) from Spain, Portugal and North Africa that it became known as *la piccola Gerusalemme*. The Jews even had their own dialect, *Guidaico Livornese* – a mixture of Hebrew and Portuguese. And they got on so well with the people of Livorno that the saying went, 'If you hurt a Jew, you harm Livorno.'

From the nineteenth century Livorno slid into decline, although many Jews still held high positions in trade and culture, maintaining close links with North Africa. By the end of World War II, however, the Sephardic community had virtually disappeared; today only a small number of Jews live in Livorno, and most are from Tunisia and Libya.

The Jewish cooking of the Italian ghettos differed from community to community. In Trieste, the cooking had a strong German and Central European influence, with a liking for dumplings, potatoes, cabbage and sweet or savoury stuffed pancakes called *palacincke*. Fruit strudels and sweet pastries, such as *putizza di noci* (chocolate almond roll) and *ofelle* (sweet crescent-shaped pastries filled with raisins, almonds and pine nuts) were also much loved.

In the Venice ghetto, the food was more varied and exotic. So much so that the Venetians soon took to the Jewish way of eating rice with all kinds of vegetables – especially artichokes, peas, courgettes (zucchini), fennel, celery, tomatoes, cabbage, potatoes and spinach. Vegetables were also often cooked *alla giudea*: simmered with raisins, pine nuts and vinegar. It was the Jews who introduced the Venetians to the aubergine (eggplant), which they had previously shunned as the 'mad apple', and to the delicious Jewish speciality of spinach croquettes with raisins and pine nuts (*polpettine di spinaci*).

Roman Jewish cooking is simple and robust. There is a liking for *fritto misto* (mixed fry) and vegetable pies (made with or without pastry) that usually include locally produced pecorino, ricotta or mozzarella; despite its name, *pizza ebraica* is not in fact a pizza, but a double-crusted pie filled with artichokes, peas and beet greens. One of the main differences between Roman and Jewish cooking is, of course, the cooking medium: traditional Roman cooking is based on pork fat, rather than olive oil.

Morocco

Jews have lived in Morocco since ancient times. The earliest
Jewish settlements were probably in the Anti-Atlas Mountains and
the Dra Valley in southern Morocco in the fifth century BC.

According to local legends, there were Jewish kingdoms and Berber tribes here long before Islam took hold in the eighth century AD. After the Arab conquest, Jewish communities sprang up all over Morocco, and by the tenth century the city of Fez was a key centre of Talmudic learning, with such a large Jewish population that it was often dubbed 'a town without people' since it appeared to have no Muslim inhabitants.

In the fifteenth century, during the Spanish Inquisition, thousands of Sephardic Jews came to Morocco, mainly settling in Fez, Meknes and Rabat: these arrivals were given the Hebrew name of *megorashim* ('the expelled'), as opposed to the native Jews or *toshavim* ('the residents'). The Jewish population of Fez became so swollen that tensions grew between Muslims and Jews, leading the sultan to move the Jews into a special quarter or mellah, next to the imperial city, for their own protection. The mellah was virtually a town unto itself, with its own laws and government, souk, gardens, synagogues and cemetery. In due course, every Moroccan city with a Jewish community had its own mellah.

When Morocco was divided between France and Spain in 1912, funds poured in from Europe to provide educational resources, and some Jews moved into newly built French colonial neighbourhoods outside the medina. By the end of World War II, there were more than 250,000 Jews living in Morocco, mainly in Casablanca, Marrakesh, Fez, Meknes, Rabat and Tangier. But after the founding of Israel in 1948, resentment between Muslims and Jews over the issue of Palestine caused many thousands of Jews to leave for Israel. Following Moroccan independence in 1956, a large part of the Jewish community moved to France and Canada.

Moroccan Jewish cuisine is among the best in the country. The Jewish repertoire is a mix of local dishes, Sephardic cooking from Spain, and Berber influences, especially in the south. Spices such as cinnamon, ginger, coriander, turmeric, saffron, and pepper are used generously; salads and sides accompany most meals, and soups are rich in legumes and vegetables. There is a liking for stuffed vegetables, fritters, and pastries called *pastels*, which are made with *warka*, a paper-thin dough. All kinds of *tajines* are enjoyed, and couscous (*seksu*) is the national dish. Couscous with seven veg (*seksu bidawi*) is served for Rosh Hashanah.

A variety of pastries is made for weddings, bar mitzvahs, circumcisions and other festive occasions – especially fried ring-shaped pastries in sugar syrup called *shebakia*, doughnuts (*sfenj*) and almond nougat (*jabane*). *Beraniya*, a kind of conserve made with fried aubergine (eggplant), is served the day after Yom Kippur.

Poland, Lithuania and Russia

From the time of the Crusades, many Ashkenazi Jews fled France and Germany and settled in Poland ('Ashkenaz' is the medieval Hebrew word for Germany).

The Jews of Germany also brought with them their Judeo-German dialect, Yiddish, which soon became the common vernacular of Jews across Central and Eastern Europe. In 1264, King Boleshaw of Poland granted protection to the Jewish community, and eventually they were given autonomy of their communal affairs.

In the middle of the sixteenth century, Poland and Lithuania were united as one country that stretched from the Baltic to the Black Sea, encompassing much of present-day Ukraine. Many Jews worked with Polish landowners, growing and exporting grain to feed the growing population of western Europe; others imported wine, textiles and luxury goods, or traded in furs.

The Polish nobility owned land in the Ukraine and employed Jews to manage their estates and collect taxes. The Jews flourished, but soon they came to be resented by the rural population, who saw them as middlemen for unjust, absentee landlords. In 1648 the Cossacks, led by Bohdan Chmielnicki, rebelled against the Polish landlords and their Jewish agents. Over the next eight years, more than 100,000 Jews were massacred, and many of the remaining Jews fled to the Balkans, Bohemia, Germany and Holland.

Towards the end of the eighteenth century, much of western Poland was partitioned to Prussia and Austria. At the same time, Russia expanded westwards and swallowed up much of eastern Poland and Lithuania. Suddenly more than a million Jews found themselves living under Russian rule. Most were confined to an area called the Pale of Settlement, which stretched roughly from Kovno and Vitebsk in the north down to Yalta on the Black Sea. A hundred years later, five million Jews were living in Russia, but a wave of pogroms in the 1880s resulted in mass emigrations: over 60,000 Jews fled to Palestine, and two million went to the Americas.

Jewish food in this region is classic Ashkenazi fare, with soups and filled pastries, especially *knishes* and *piroshki*. Crepes like buckwheat blini and filled blintzes are popular, as are all kinds of dumplings, such as matzo-meal *kneidlach*, potato dumplings (*kartoffel klishkes*), and *kreplach*, a sort of ravioli usually served in broth. One of the most well known Ashkenazi dishes is *kasha varnishkes* (buckwheat with bow-tie pasta). Pickles are generally on the table, including sauerkraut, cucumber and *tzikel* – beetroot (beets). Dairy products are a staple, especially sour cream, buttermilk, curd and cream cheese. Fruit compotes are served for desserts, especially on the Sabbath, and strudels, cheesecakes, honey cakes, apple cakes and poppy seed rolls are made for festivals. *Lokschen kugel* (sweet noodle pudding), *honig leiker* (honey cake) and *teiglach* (pellets of dough cooked in honey syrup) are served during Rosh Hashanah.

Romania

Jews first came to Romania in Roman times, followed by Khazar Jews in the tenth century, Ashkenazim expelled from Hungary in 1367, Sephardic exiles from Spain in 1492, and a wave of Polish and Ukrainian Jews after the Chmielnicki massacres in 1648.

Further waves of Jewish immigrants from Poland and Russia continued into the nineteenth century.

By the 1930s, there were more than 800,000 Jews living in Romania, mostly in Transylvania, Bessarabia and Moldavia – and especially in Bukovina, where they prospered as craftsmen and small traders. Some Jews lived in self-sufficient rural communities (Romania was one of the few countries where Jews were allowed to own land), and in Bucharest, a small number of Sephardic Jews played an active role in business and financial life.

After World War II, Romania became part of the Soviet Union until the Revolution of 1989. During that time, around 300,000 Jews emigrated to Israel. Nevertheless around 20,000 Jews still live in Romania – in Bucharest, Chisinau and in small communities scattered around the country.

Romanian Jewish cuisine is strongly influenced by both Ashkenazi and Sephardic traditions, as well as Hungarian, Russian, French and especially Turkish cooking; the Turks brought corn from the New World to Romania, and it is still a staple food today. There is a taste for *ciorbe* – vegetable soups with a tangy, tart flavour designed to whet the appetite. Romanians also enjoy sweet and savoury pancakes (*clatite*) and dumplings (*papanasi, galuste* or *galushkas*), often topped with tomato sauce and grated cheese and baked in the oven. Vegetarian dishes of note include fried peppers stuffed with cheese (*pipirushkas reyenados de keso*), vegetable rissoles (*parjoale de legume*) and a mixed vegetable stew called *ghiveci*.

Romanian desserts such as baklava, *konafa* and sponge cake (*pandispan*) reflect Turkish and Sephardic influences.

Spain and Portugal

After the Destruction of the First Temple in 586 BC, many Jews
went to live in Spain, especially around Cordoba in the south.
Before the Arab conquest in AD 711 , Jews had been subjected to
more than a hundred years of persecution by the Visigoths.

However, under Muslim rule many rose to
prominence as government administrators,
lawyers, doctors, financiers and philosophers.
Jewish merchants, bookbinders and tailors also
flourished, and some Jews owned vineyards and
olive groves.

Soon Jewish communities sprang up in all
the major cities of Al-Andalus, which at its
height covered much of modern-day Spain and
Portugal. The Jews became an integral part of
Muslim society, speaking Arabic and adopting
Arab dress; however, things began to change
in the eleventh century. This was the time of
the Reconquista, the re-conquering of Spain
by the Christian states to the north, and by the
beginning of the thirteenth century, all of Spain
except for Granada was under Christian rule.
At this time, what remained of Al-Andalus was
still ruled by the Berbers, who tried to force Jews
to convert to Islam, prompting many to flee to
northern Spain and what is now Portugal. At
first they were treated well, but this changed at
the end of the fourteenth century when angry
Christian mobs destroyed the Jewish quarters
of Seville, Barcelona, Cordoba and Toledo.
Thousands of Jews were massacred and many
more fled; others were forcibly converted to
Christianity but practised Judaism in secret,
and came to be known as *conversos* or *marranos*
(literally meaning 'pork', as they were forced to

eat pork in public to demonstrate their disregard
for Jewish dietary laws).

Finally, in 1492, the Spanish Inquisition saw
the expulsion of all Jews from Spain, as well
as the Spanish colonies in southern Italy,
Sicily, Sardinia, Provence and the New World.
Most fled to Greece and Turkey; some went to
Holland, France, Italy and North Africa; and
others – mainly *conversos* – managed to board
ships with the Conquistadors. Many ended up in
Mexico and Brazil, while others escaped to Peru.

As most Spanish Jews fled to the Ottoman
Empire after the Inquisition, the traditional
cooking of the Sephardim is probably more
accurately reflected in the Jewish cooking of
Greece and Turkey than in that of Spain – with
one important difference, the exclusion of
foods from the New World, such as tomatoes,
potatoes, corn, sweet (bell) peppers, hot chillies,
pumpkins, beans and chocolate.

Nevertheless, there are some early records
of Jewish dishes in Spain – found mainly in
Inquisition tribunals and early cookbooks, such
as Roberto de Nola's *Libre de Coch*, printed in
1477. As in most Mediterranean countries, the
diet was based on wheat, olives and wine. In the
eighth century, the Moors introduced a wide
variety of new foods into Iberia, especially rice,
sugar, oranges, capers, artichokes and aubergines

(eggplants), as well as all kinds of spices, including saffron, ginger, cumin, cinnamon and cardamom. Vegetable stews and casseroles (*ollas*) were made with eggs and cheese, hard-boiled eggs were roasted overnight over hot coals (*huevos asados* or *huevos haminados*), and stews of chickpeas (*olla de garbanzos*) or chickpeas with spinach (*hamin de berzas*) were usually prepared for the Sabbath. Vegetables, especially onions, were often served *con almodrote* – in a sauce based on cheese, hard-boiled egg yolks, breadcrumbs, garlic, olive oil and vegetable broth, according to de Nola.

Fresh fruit was usually eaten for dessert, but Spanish Jews also had a liking for candied fruit and sweetmeats made with ground nuts, especially dried figs stuffed with almonds or walnuts (*empanadas de igos*). They also made a variety of sweet fritters and pastries soaked in honey, such as *bunuelos* and *rosquillas*.

Syria

Jews have lived in Syria for more than 2,000 years. Most were Mizrachim who never left the Middle East, but some were Sephardim who fled the Spanish Inquisition in 1492.

Aleppo had been an important base for the ancient caravan trade between the Middle East and the Orient since the Middle Ages, and it continued to flourish as a centre of international trade right up until the middle of the nineteenth century.

When the Suez Canal opened in 1869, the caravan routes lost their importance and many Jewish merchants found themselves without a livelihood. This began the first wave of migrations: some Jews went to Cairo to continue trading from there; others emigrated to England and North America. After the Young Turk Revolution in 1908, many young Jewish men fled Syria with their families, in order to avoid conscription into the army. Some left for Egypt,

some settled in England and the United States, especially New York and along the New Jersey coast; others went to Mexico, Panama, Brazil and Argentina. After the formation of the state of Israel in 1948, many Syrian Jews crossed the border into Israel.

The Jewish cuisine of Aleppo was renowned: a mix of Arabic, Turkish, Persian and Sephardic influences, characterized by spices such as cinnamon, allspice and cumin, and the piquant flavours of tamarind and pomegranate molasses. Most meals included a variety of delicious *mezze*, such as hummus, roasted aubergine (eggplant) with tahini (*baba ghanouj*), and vine leaves stuffed with rice and mint (*yebrah hamaud*). Bulgur was a staple, although the wealthy Jewish middle classes preferred white rice, which was often cooked with vermicelli (*wa shariyya*) – or, for special occasions, with almonds or pistachios (*wa loz*). Lentils and rice with caramelized onions (*mujaddara*) was often served for supper on Thursday evenings. All kinds of omelettes and fritters (*ejjeh*) were made with courgettes (zucchini), leeks, Swiss chard, potatoes, parsley and fresh cheese; and the Sephardim introduced *pastels* – savoury pastries, usually filled with spinach or cheese. Fresh fruit or dried fruit and nuts were generally served for dessert, with sweet pastries soaked in sugar syrup, such as baklava and *konafa*, enjoyed by Jews and Syrians alike. Sesame seed candies flavoured with ginger and cinnamon (*simsemiyeh*) were usually served for Rosh Hashanah.

Tunisia and Algeria

Jews are thought to have arrived in Tunisia and Algeria with Phoenician traders, during the reign of King Solomon. In Roman times, there were scattered Jewish communities along the coast of North Africa, mainly involved in agriculture and trade.

And legend has it that Kahina, a Jewish Berber queen and prophetess, led the last Berber resistance against the Arab invasion of the Maghreb in the seventh century.

One of the earliest Jewish communities in Tunisia settled on the island of Djerba, where locals claim that the synagogue of El Ghriba ('the miracle') occupies the site of one of the oldest synagogues in the world, built where a holy stone fell from heaven. The Jews of Djerba have retained their own distinct form of Judaism, virtually untouched by outside influences.

After the Spanish Inquisition in 1492, thousands of Sephardim fled to North Africa. Some settled in Algeria, while others went on to Tunisia, especially Tunis and Testour, where they built houses in the Andalusian style, with tiled inner courtyards and balconies. By the end of the sixteenth century, Algeria, Tunisia and Tripolitana (present-day Libya) were under Ottoman rule. Soon after, a large contingent of Jews from Livorno came to Algiers and Tunis to negotiate ransoms for Jews kidnapped by local pirates. The new arrivals were encouraged to stay by local *beys* (governors), and many Livornese prospered as merchants, bankers and traders because of their close connections with Europe. However, the majority of the Jewish community struggled to earn a living as peddlers, tailors, embroiderers, shoemakers, carpenters, goldsmiths, silversmiths, jewellers and money-changers. By the end of the eighteenth century, most Jews lived in a *hara* (Jewish quarter), in exceptionally overcrowded and seriously impoverished conditions.

Life did not improve until the French took over Algeria in 1831, and then Tunisia fifty years later. Many Jews thrived under the burgeoning economy of the new French Protectorates, and some were able to leave the hara and move into more comfortable apartments in the French quarter. Most Algerian Jews were given French nationality. Just before Algeria gained independence, in 1962, about 150,000 people (almost the entire Jewish population) emigrated to France. After Tunisian independence, in 1956, about 40,000 Jews moved to Israel and France.

Tunisian Jews are very proud of their cuisine, which has French, Italian, Andalusian and Ottoman influences. Meals usually begin with a *kemia*: a selection of small cooked vegetable salads, such as roast peppers, tomatoes and garlic (*mechouia*); spicy carrot salad (*mzora*); and artichokes with harissa, the fiery North African condiment made with dried chillies, garlic and spices. They are also fond of stuffed vegetables, vegetable fritters and deep-fried savoury pastries called *briks*. Tunisian soups are rich in vegetables and pulses, and often include homemade pasta, such as *reuchtas* (noodles) or *noissars* (squares of egg pasta). Traditional dairy dishes include a variety of baked omelettes (*makhouda*), usually made with potatoes, carrots or aubergines (eggplants), scrambled

eggs in a spicy sauce (*ojja*), and fried vegetables cooked with eggs (*chakchouka*).

Cakes and pastries, such as *manicottis* (fried pastry rosettes) and *yoyos* (little doughnuts), are usually soaked in honey or sugar syrup. And when the Livornese Jews came to Tunisia, they brought *scoudilini* (a rich almond custard) and *boca di dama* (almond sponge cake) with them.

Vegetables have always played an important role in Algerian Jewish cooking. All kinds of cooked salads are prepared for the Sabbath: artichokes, fennel, celery, cucumber, roasted aubergines (eggplants), tomatoes, peppers, carrots and courgettes (zucchini), usually dressed with olive oil, lemon juice, garlic, harissa, ground caraway seeds and coriander. One of the most popular vegetarian dishes is *loubia* (white beans simmered in a spicy sauce), which is traditionally served for Sukkot, while *boketof* (a vegetable soup flavoured with mint) is often served for the festival of Tisha Be-Av.

Couscous is a staple and is often served simply with butter, raisins, sugar and a glass of *iben* (buttermilk). *Boureks* or *bestels*, deep-fried sweet or savoury pastries similar to the *briks* of Tunisia, are usually made for weddings and other special occasions. Some of the better-known desserts include *cigares aux amandes* (fried paper-thin pastries filled with almond paste and soaked in honey syrup), *knidlets* (almond pastries) and *el baghrir* (spongy semolina pancakes served with an orange blossom syrup).

Turkey and Greece

It is not known when the first Jews settled in Greece and Turkey,
but by the end of the first century BC there were thriving Jewish
communities in most of the cities and principalities of Asia Minor,
as well as on Crete, Cyprus and some of the Aegean islands.

Under Roman rule, Jews were free to practise their religion, but were not allowed to participate in public life.

After AD 330, when Constantine the Great moved the imperial capital to Byzantium (and renamed it Constantinople), the Eastern Roman Empire came to be known as the Byzantine Empire – but the Jews of Byzantium were proud of Rome and its civilization and thought of themselves as Romans, and so came to be known as Romaniote Jews.

Then, in the early thirteenth century, Crete, the Ionian Islands and some of the Aegean Islands came under Venetian rule, an influence still apparent today – not only in the many Venetian castles and buildings, but also in the cuisine. The *fritole* (rice fritters) of Corfu and the Cretan *sofegada* – aubergine (eggplant), courgette (zucchini) and pepper stew – both have obvious Venetian origins.

In 1453 the Ottoman Turks conquered Constantinople and, over the next two centuries, most of Greece. Ottoman rule lasted for more than 400 years, with life improving for the Jews, since Christians and Jews were treated alike. After the Spanish Inquisition, Sultan Beyazit II opened the empire's borders to the Jews fleeing Spain, and thousands settled in Constantinople, Izmir, Edirne and especially Thessaloniki – which, by the end of the sixteenth century, was predominantly Jewish, so much so that it became known as 'the Jerusalem of the Balkans'.

The Spanish Jews, or Sephardim (the names derives from *sepharad*, the Hebrew word for spain), brought their own sophisticated culture and cuisine with them. Most spoke Castilian Spanish, which gradually developed into Ladino or Judesmo (a mixture of Spanish and loan words from Hebrew, Greek, Turkish, Italian and Arabic), and this soon became the *lingua franca* of the Jews of Greece and Turkey. Among their number were bankers, doctors, interpreters and printers, and many went into government office; others became merchants, trading in silks, precious stones, coffee, and spices.

By the end of the nineteenth century, the Ottoman Empire had gone into decline. After Greece entered World War I in 1917, a fire swept through Thessaloniki, destroying most of the Jewish quarter. As a result, many of the city's Jews moved to Athens or emigrated to France, Africa, the United States and South America. When the Nazis invaded Greece in World War II, more than 65,000 Jews were sent to concentration camps. Today there are about 6,000 Jews in Greece – and about 20,000 Jews in Turkey, most of them in Istanbul.

The cuisine of Greek and Turkish Jews has been strongly influenced by Sephardic and Ottoman cooking, with dishes such as *empanadas* (savoury turnovers) having obvious Spanish origins. There is a liking for pickled vegetables (*tursi*) and a range of savoury pastries (*bourekas, boyos, pastels, tapadas* and *bulemas*) filled with spinach, Swiss chard, eggplant (aubergine), potato, pumpkin or cheese. Some of the most well known of the vast repertoire of vegetarian dishes include Swiss chard and potato pie (*sfongo de pazi*), a courgette (zucchini) and white cheese gratin called *kalavasutcho*, and sweet (bell) peppers or tomatoes stuffed with rice, pine nuts and currants. Leek and white cheese fritters (*albondigas de prasa*), a spinach and matzo gratin called *mina de smyrne*, and a variety of vegetable omelettes (*fritadas*) are traditionally served for Passover.

A large number of cakes and pastries are made, many of them soaked in syrup, such as *tishpishti* (a light walnut cake often prepared for Rosh Hashanah), the rich custard-filled pastry known as *galaktoboureko*, and baklava. Greek honey puffs (*zvingous*) and sweet fritters called *bimuelos de hanuka* are traditionally made for Chanukah.

Appetizers
and salads

'An empty stomach – a heart without joy'

JUDEO-SPANISH PROVERB

All around the Mediterranean and the Middle East, meals begin with a variety of appetizers and salads called antipasti, mezze or kemia. These are especially important in Jewish households because of the Sabbath laws, which forbid the cooking of food on the Sabbath. North African Jews in particular have an enormous repertoire of raw and cooked salads, made with artichokes, courgettes (zucchini), fennel, peppers, tomatoes, cauliflower, carrots, potatoes or broad (fava) beans, and often dressed with olive oil, lemon juice, garlic, cumin and harissa – the spicy hot sauce that is so popular throughout the Maghreb.

Across Eastern Europe and Russia, salads of beetroots (beets), potatoes or cabbage predominate – usually dressed with sour cream and herbs. In Georgia, salads of beans, beetroots (beets), mushrooms or aubergines (eggplants) often include walnuts or pomegranate seeds, while in Iran and the Balkans, vegetable salads are often mixed with yoghurt.

Middle Eastern mezze are not only served as appetizers, but can also make up an entire meal. A typical combination might be a bowl of hummus, the parsley and bulgur salad called tabbouleh, several kinds of olives, raw vegetables such as carrot, celery or cucumber, stuffed vegetables and perhaps some goat's cheese.

Sabbath artichoke salad with fennel and harissa

Salade d'artichauts cuits du Chabbat

4 medium artichokes

½ lemon

3 tablespoons extra virgin olive oil

225g (8oz) small white onions, peeled but left whole

3 garlic cloves, finely chopped

1 medium fennel bulb, trimmed and cut into thin wedges

½ teaspoon tomato puree (paste)

1 teaspoon harissa (see recipe), or to taste

about 125ml (½ cup) hot water

For the harissa

60g (2oz) dried red chillies

1 small head of garlic, cloves separated and peeled

1 teaspoon toasted and ground coriander seeds

1 teaspoon toasted and ground caraway seeds

½ teaspoon salt

2 tablespoons extra virgin olive oil, plus extra for storing

In this recipe from Tunis, artichokes are simmered with baby onions, fennel and harissa and served at room temperature. Harissa is a hot sauce based on dried chillies, garlic and salt that is widely used as a condiment in North Africa. It is readily available at most supermarkets or Middle Eastern stores, but the strength can vary considerably, so you may need to adjust the amount used according to taste. Harissa is also very easy to prepare at home. Always use rubber gloves when handling chillies, and avoid any contact with the eyes.

—

To make the harissa, remove the seeds and stalks from the chillies and place in a bowl. Cover with boiling water and leave to soak for 30 minutes, until the chillies are soft. Drain, then place in a food processor with the garlic, spices, salt and 2 tablespoons of olive oil. Process to a smooth paste. Spoon the harissa into a sterilized glass jar, and cover with a layer of olive oil. It will keep in the refrigerator for up to 2 weeks.

Trim and peel the stems of the artichokes, then remove all the outer tough, inedible leaves. Cut the artichokes in half and remove the fuzzy chokes. Rub the artichoke bottoms all over with the lemon half to prevent them from blackening, then cut into 5mm (¼in) slices.

Heat the olive oil in a large frying pan and cook the onions and garlic for 2 minutes. Add the fennel and artichokes, then stir in the tomato puree and harissa. Pour over the hot water and bring to the boil. Cover, then turn down to a simmer and cook for 20-25 minutes or until the vegetables are tender and the sauce has thickened. Transfer to a serving dish and serve at room temperature.

Serves 4

Jewish caponata

Caponata alla giudea

675g (1½lb) aubergines (eggplants)

2 tablespoons olive oil, plus more for frying

1 small onion, finely chopped

1 celery stalk, cut into small dice

1 small carrot, cut into very small dice

225g (8oz) ripe plum tomatoes, peeled, deseeded and chopped

75g (⅔ cup) green olives, pitted and sliced

3 tablespoons salted capers, well rinsed

2 tablespoons torn basil leaves

3 tablespoons red wine vinegar, or to taste

1 tablespoon sugar

salt and freshly ground black pepper

1 hard-boiled egg, sliced

This dish consists of fried aubergine (eggplant) in a sweet and sour tomato sauce flavoured with olives and capers. The dish originated in Sicily, but was brought to Rome by Sicilian Jews fleeing the Inquisition. Traditionally, caponata was made on Fridays and served cold for lunch on the Sabbath.

—

Trim the ends off the aubergines, then cut into 1cm (½in) dice and sprinkle with salt. Place in a colander set over a bowl and leave for 1 hour to drain off any bitter juices. Rinse off the salt and pat dry, then fry in hot olive oil until golden. Drain on paper towels.

Heat the 2 tablespoons olive oil in a large frying pan and cook the onion, celery and carrot over a moderate heat until soft. Add the tomatoes and continue to cook until the sauce has thickened. Stir in the fried aubergines, olives and capers and simmer for 5 minutes. Add the basil, vinegar and sugar and stir well, then season with salt and pepper and simmer for a further 5 minutes to blend the flavours. Transfer to a serving dish and garnish with sliced hard-boiled egg. Serve at room temperature.

Serves 4

Beetroot salad with horseradish, sour cream and dill

Salat iz svekly s khrenom

4 medium beetroots (beets), about 675g (1½lb)

3 tablespoons red wine vinegar, or to taste

pinch of ground cinnamon

2–3 tablespoons freshly grated horseradish root, or to taste

125ml (½ cup) sour cream or smetana

1 teaspoon sugar, or to taste

salt

2 tablespoons finely chopped dill (or parsley)

Variations of this salad are made all over Eastern Europe. Be warned that peeling and grating horseradish root might bring tears to your eyes – but it will also clear your sinuses! Fresh horseradish is best for this recipe, but if it is unavailable you can use ready-grated horseradish instead, but it does not have the fiery heat.

—

Wash the beetroots well and trim the ends. Place in a saucepan of cold water and bring to the boil. Cover and simmer for about 1 hour or until tender, then drain and set aside until cool enough to handle. Peel and slice thinly. Place in a salad bowl and pour over the vinegar. Add the cinnamon, toss lightly, and leave to marinate for 30 minutes.

Mix the horseradish and sour cream in a small bowl and season with sugar and salt. Pour over the marinated beetroot and garnish with dill.

Serves 4

Broad bean falafel

Ta'miya

350g (2 cups) dried ful nabed or dried skinless split broad (fava) beans

handful of flat-leaf parsley

handful of coriander (cilantro)

2 spring onions (scallions), chopped

3 garlic cloves, crushed

2 teaspoons ground coriander

1 teaspoon ground cumin

$\frac{1}{4}$ teaspoon cayenne pepper

$\frac{1}{2}$ teaspoon bicarbonate of soda (baking soda)

salt and freshly ground black pepper

3–4 tablespoons sesame seeds

olive oil, for deep-frying

Ta'miya, or falafel, have been made in Egypt since the days of the Pharaohs, when they were probably enjoyed as much by Jewish slaves as they were by the Egyptians. Today both Egypt and Israel claim these tasty fritters as their own. In Egypt they are always made with *ful nabed* (white broad beans), whereas in Israel they are prepared with chickpeas. Sometimes *ta'miya* are lightly coated in sesame seeds, which gives them a delicious, nutty flavour. In Egypt, they are traditionally served stuffed inside warm pita bread with a little chopped cucumber and tomato salad and a dollop of hummus.

—

Soak the beans in plenty of water for 24 hours. Drain well and pat dry in a tea towel.

Wash the herbs and dry them thoroughly. Chop coarsely.

Place the beans in a blender or food processor and process to a smooth, soft paste. Add the spring onions, garlics, herbs, spices and bicarbonate of soda and process again until the mixture is very smooth. Season with salt and pepper, then transfer to a bowl and refrigerate for 1 hour before using.

Shape the mixture into small balls about 2cm ($\frac{3}{4}$in) in diameter. Flatten the balls slightly and roll them in sesame seeds. Working in batches, deep-fry in hot oil until golden on both sides. Remove with a slotted spoon and drain on paper towels.

Serves 6–8

Beetroot salad with pomegranate molasses and sesame seeds

Sa'lata shooendar

4 medium beetroots (beets), about 675g (1½lb)

1 small red onion, finely chopped

a handful of finely chopped flat-leaf parsley

3 tablespoons extra virgin olive oil

juice of ½ lemon

1 garlic clove, crushed

1–2 teaspoons pomegranate molasses, to taste

salt and freshly ground black pepper

2 tablespoons toasted sesame seeds

Pomegranate molasses, made by reducing and concentrating the juice of pomegranates, adds a delicious, slightly tart flavour to savoury stews and salad dressings. It's available in most Middle Eastern stores, but comes in various densities, so the exact amount needed will depend on the thickness of your molasses. This salad will keep for up to 3 days in the refrigerator.

—

Wash the beetroots well and trim the ends. Place in a saucepan of cold water and bring to the boil. Cover and simmer for about 1 hour or until tender, then drain and set aside until cool enough to handle. Peel and slice. Place in a salad bowl, together with the onion and parsley.

To make a dressing for the salad, combine the olive oil, lemon juice, crushed garlic and pomegranate molasses in a small glass jar. Season with salt and pepper and shake well. Pour over the beetroot and toss lightly, then garnish with sesame seeds and serve cold.

Serves 4

Liptoi cheese

Korozott liptoi

225g (8oz) cottage cheese

6 tablespoons softened butter

2 tablespoons sour cream

2 tablespoons finely grated onion

1 tablespoon Hungarian paprika

½ teaspoon ground caraway seeds

salt and freshly ground black pepper

This well-known cheese spread is much loved by Hungarians and Jews alike. It originated in the county of Lipto in northern Hungary, where the famous sheep's curd cheese of the region is mixed with softened butter, grated onion, paprika and caraway seeds. Variations of this dish are made all over Central Europe – some cooks like to add a little prepared mustard. In Vienna, where it is called *liptauer*, chives and capers are often added. Serve with quarters of rye bread or toast, or as a dip for raw vegetables.

—

Sieve the cheese into a bowl, add the softened butter and sour cream and combine thoroughly. Add the onion, paprika and caraway and mix well. Season with salt and pepper, then refrigerate for 2–3 hours to let the flavours blend.

Serves 4

Hummus with whole chickpeas and sumac
Hummus bi tahina

225g (1½ cups) cooked and drained chickpeas

juice 1–1½ lemons, to taste

2–3 tablespoons tahini, to taste

1–2 garlic cloves, crushed

2 tablespoons extra virgin olive oil

¼ teaspoon ground cumin

salt

1 teaspoon sumac

No Jewish cookbook would be complete without a recipe for hummus. It is made all over Israel and the Middle East – and in recent years throughout most of the western world. If you have a food processor or blender it is surprisingly easy to prepare at home, and the exact amount of tahini, garlic and lemon juice can be varied according to your taste. It is traditionally served with warm pita bread, but it is also very good as a dip for raw vegetables. Sometimes the hummus is topped with whole chickpeas, a drizzle of olive oil and a sprinkling of paprika or sumac, which gives it a delicious tangy flavour. If using canned chickpeas rinse them well under cold water to remove the salt.

—

Reserve 3 tablespoons of chickpeas for the garnish. Place the remaining chickpeas, lemon juice, tahini, garlic, 6 tablespoons water and 2 tablespoons of the olive oil in a food processor and process until smooth and creamy. If the mixture is too thick, thin it with a little more water. Add the cumin and season with salt, then spread over a shallow serving dish. Drizzle over the remaining olive oil and sprinkle with sumac. Garnish with the reserved chickpeas.

Serves 3–4

Sephardic cheese and parsley pastries
Borekitas de kezo

4–5 large sheets fresh or thawed frozen filo pastry

extra virgin olive oil, for brushing

3 tablespoons nigella seeds

For the filling

200g (1 cup) mashed feta or beyaz peynir (Turkish white cheese)

75g (1 cup) freshly grated parmesan or kefalotyri cheese

1 egg, plus 1 yolk

25g (1 cup) finely chopped flat-leaf parsley

2 tablespoons finely chopped mint

These delicious little pastries are traditionally served for the Sabbath brunch and for Shavuot, but they are also very good with aperitifs. Nigella seeds add a spicy, almost onion-like flavour. Any other filling for Sephardic pastries in this book, such as *bulemas*, *pastels* or *filas*, can be used to make *borekitas*.

—

To make the filling, combine both the cheeses, egg, egg yolk and herbs in a bowl and mix well.

Cut the filo pastry into strips approximately 6cm ($2\frac{1}{2}$in) wide and 30cm (12in) long. Place in a pile and cover with a clean cloth to prevent them from drying out. Take one strip of filo pastry and brush lightly with oil. Place about 1 teaspoon of filling over the bottom end of the pastry strip. Carefully lift up the right-hand corner and fold over to make a triangle. Fold over and over again until you have reached the top. Repeat with the remaining filo strips and filling.

Place the filo pastry triangles side by side on a greased baking sheet and brush the tops lightly with oil. Sprinkle with nigella seeds and bake in a preheated 180°C/350°F/gas 4 oven for 15 minutes or until crisp and golden.

Makes about 24

Marinated green beans with balsamic dressing

Fagiolini all'aceto

450g (1lb) green beans

3 tablespoons extra virgin olive oil

1 tablespoon balsamic vinegar

1 teaspoon cream of balsamic vinegar (optional)

about 90ml ($\frac{1}{3}$ cup) hot water

salt and freshly ground black pepper

This Italian dish may be eaten as an appetizer or side dish. In Ferrara, they make this using the tiny green beans that are available in early June. I like to add a little cream of balsamic vinegar (crema di aceto di balsamic di Modena), which has added grape must and gives the dressing a delicious flavour.

—

Top and tail the green beans. Heat the olive oil in a large frying pan and add the beans, stirring well to coat them in oil and vinegar, if using. Pour in the hot water and bring to the boil. Cover and simmer for 15 minutes or until the beans are tender and the liquid has evaporated. Season with salt and pepper, then serve at room temperature.

Serves 4

Green peppers with argan oil

Felfla bi argane

6 green (bell) peppers

3 tablespoons argan oil or extra virgin olive oil

juice of $\frac{1}{2}$ lemon

2 garlic cloves, finely chopped

$\frac{1}{4}$ teaspoon ground cumin

$\frac{1}{4}$ teaspoon paprika

salt and freshly ground black pepper

The rare argan or ironwood tree only grows in southern Morocco, in the region around Essaouira, the old city of Mogador, which once had a large Jewish community. The amber-coloured oil is made from the tree's oleaginous nuts and has a slightly nutty, peppery taste that is more subtle than olive oil. Although argan oil's high smoking point means it can be used for cooking, it is mostly drizzled over salads, vegetable dishes, couscous and bread.

—

Roast the peppers under a hot grill (broiler) until blackened all over. Rinse under cold water and remove the skins. Cut in half and remove the seeds and core. Cut into strips and place in a serving bowl.

Make a dressing by whisking together the oil, lemon juice, garlic and spices. Season with salt and pepper, then pour over the peppers and toss lightly. Leave to marinate for at least an hour. Serve cold.

Serves 4–6

Sweet and sour small white onions

Cipolline in agrodolce

5 tablespoons extra virgin olive oil

675g (1½lb) small white onions, peeled but left whole

2 tablespoons sugar, or to taste

2 tablespoons red wine vinegar

75g (½ cup) sultanas (golden raisins)

2 tablespoons dry marsala

about 4 tablespoons hot water

salt and freshly ground black pepper

In this classic Sabbath dish, onions are simmered with sultanas (golden raisins) in a delicious sweet and sour sauce made with sugar, red wine vinegar and marsala.

—

Heat the olive oil in a large frying pan and add the onions. Cover and cook over a gentle heat for about 25 minutes or until the onions start to soften.

Dissolve the sugar in the vinegar, then add to the pan, along with the sultanas, marsala and the hot water. Stir well and season with salt and pepper. Simmer for a further 40 minutes or until the onions are golden and the sauce is caramelized. Transfer to a serving dish and serve chilled.

Serves 4–6

Parsley, tomato and bulgur salad with fresh mint

Tabbouleh

50g (2oz) fine bulgur

75g (3 cups) flat-leaf parsley, leaves picked and finely chopped

15g ($\frac{1}{2}$ cup) mint, leaves picked and finely chopped

3 spring onions (scallions), finely chopped

4 medium tomatoes, cored and cut into 5mm ($\frac{1}{4}$in) dice

6 tablespoons extra virgin olive oil

juice of 1 lemon, or to taste

$\frac{1}{2}$ teaspoon ground allspice

$\frac{1}{4}$ teaspoon ground cinnamon

salt and freshly ground black pepper

seeds of $\frac{1}{2}$ pomegranate

The proportions of the ingredients in this delicious salad from Aleppo vary from cook to cook. Most Syrian Jews like to make it with a large amount of bulgur, but I find the result lighter and more delicious with less. Tabbouleh is usually served with crisp lettuce or cabbage leaves, which are used to scoop up the salad.

—

Place the bulgur in a bowl, cover with cold water and leave to soak for 10 minutes. Drain well, squeezing out as much excess water as possible. Place in a bowl, along with the herbs, spring onions and tomatoes.

Make a dressing by whisking the olive oil with the lemon juice, then add the spices and season with salt and pepper.

Pour the dressing over the salad and toss lightly. Garnish with pomegranate seeds and serve.

Serves 4

Pepper and tomato jam
Makbouba

450g (1lb) tomatoes

2–3 red or green (bell) peppers, about 350g (12oz)

3 tablespoons extra virgin olive oil

2 garlic cloves, finely chopped

$\frac{1}{4}$ teaspoon ground cumin

1 bay leaf

a sprig of thyme

salt and freshly ground black pepper

This delicious Judeo-Arab dish consists of roast tomatoes and peppers slowly simmered in olive oil with garlic and herbs until they are almost the consistency of marmalade. Sometimes a little ground caraway or cumin is added. *Makbouba* is usually served at room temperature with warm flat bread, but it can also be used to stuff eggs or as a sauce for pasta.

—

Roast the tomatoes and peppers under a hot grill (broiler) until blackened all over. Rinse under cold water and remove the skins. Cut in half and remove the seeds. Cut the peppers into strips and roughly chop the tomatoes.

Heat the olive oil in a large frying pan, add the garlic and cook for 1 minute. Add the cumin, bay leaf, thyme, peppers and tomatoes. Season with salt and pepper, then simmer, uncovered, for about 1 hour or until the liquid has evaporated and the sauce has reduced to a jam-like consistency. Serve cold.

Serves 4

Orange and black olive salad

Salade d'oranges et d'olives noires

3–4 oranges

20 black olives, pitted and halved

2 tablespoons extra virgin olive oil

1–2 teaspoons lemon juice, to taste

1 garlic clove, crushed

½ teaspoon paprika

½ teaspoon ground cumin

pinch of sugar

salt

This refreshing salad is often served for Tu Bi-Shevat, the Festival of the Trees.

—

Peel the oranges, taking care to remove all the pith, then cut into small dice. Place the oranges and olives in a serving bowl.

To make a dressing for the salad, mix the olive oil, lemon juice, garlic, spices and sugar in a small bowl and season with salt. Pour over the oranges and olives and toss lightly. Chill thoroughly before serving.

Serves 4

Tomato, onion and egg salad

Slata tomatem

450g (1lb) tomatoes, diced

1 small red onion, thinly sliced

100g (¾ cup) black olives, pitted

3 tablespoons extra virgin olive oil

1 tablespoon red wine vinegar

3 garlic cloves, crushed

salt and freshly ground black pepper

2 tablespoons finely chopped flat-leaf parsley

2 hard-boiled eggs, sliced

This simple salad makes a delicious appetizer or a light lunch with some bread on the side.

—

Place the tomatoes, onion and olives in a bowl. To make a dressing for the salad, whisk together the olive oil, vinegar and garlic. Season with salt and pepper, then pour over the salad and toss lightly. Garnish with parsley and hard-boiled eggs.

Serves 4

Potato salad with apple, capers and dill pickles

Bramborovy salat

675g (1½lb) new potatoes

1 small apple, peeled, cored and diced

1 small onion, finely chopped

1–2 gherkins or dill pickles, chopped

2 teaspoons capers

2 tablespoons finely chopped flat-leaf parsley

4 tablespoons mayonnaise

2 tablespoons sour cream or smetana

1 teaspoon wholegrain mustard

salt and freshly ground black pepper

1 hard-boiled egg, chopped

All kinds of potato salads are made by Ashkenazi Jews, especially for the Sabbath. Sometimes a little diced cucumber or celery is added, or some cooked carrot, beetroot (beets) or peas. The dressing can vary from a simple vinaigrette or mayonnaise to a mixture of sour cream and mustard. In this recipe from Prague, the salad is dressed with mayonnaise and sour cream or smetana – a cultured cream similar to crème fraîche that is widely used in cooking all over Central and Eastern Europe.

—

Cook the potatoes in their skins in lightly salted water for 20 minutes or until tender. Drain and leave until cool enough to handle, then peel if necessary – there's no need to peel small new potatoes. Cut the potatoes into thick slices or large dice. Add the apple, onion, gherkin, capers and parsley.

In a small bowl, mix together the mayonnaise, sour cream and mustard. Season with salt and pepper, then pour over the potato salad and toss lightly. Serve cold, garnished with hard-boiled egg.

Serves 4

Soups

'Worries go down better with soup.'

YIDDISH SAYING

Soups have always been important in the Jewish kitchen. In medieval France and Germany, soups were usually served at every meal, and in poorer households a meal would often consist simply of soup with bread – in fact, the word 'soup' derives from the German *sup*, which originally referred to a piece of bread soaked in liquid.

Soup also plays an essential part in many Jewish holidays and festivals. Russian *borsch*, Lithuanian *krupnik* or Italian *minestrone del Sabato* were traditionally served for Friday night dinner. Soups are often simmered slowly overnight and served for lunch on the Sabbath. Moroccan Jews like to prepare harira, a soup rich in pulses, for Yom Kippur, while Algerian Jews serve a vegetable and vermicelli soup called *boketof* to break the fast of Tisha Be-Av.

Jewish soups generally fall into four categories: cold soups, such as the chilled fruit soups of Central and Eastern Europe; simple soups or broths made with water or stock that often include dumplings; pureed soups, usually enriched with sour cream or yoghurt; and substantial soups made with grains and pulses that are meals in themselves.

Chilled cucumber and yoghurt soup with fresh mint

Ab-doogh kheeyah

4 baby cucumbers

400g (2 cups) strained yoghurt

about 225ml (scant 1 cup) iced water

1 garlic clove, crushed (optional)

2 tablespoons finely chopped chives

2 tablespoons finely chopped dill

2 tablespoons finely chopped mint

salt and freshly ground black pepper

Variations of this refreshing summer soup are made all over the Middle and Near East. Sometimes sultanas (golden raisins) and walnuts are added, or spring onions (scallions) are substituted for the chives. Some cooks like to add a few ice cubes to the soup just before serving. The small un-waxed cucumbers found in Middle Eastern stores are best for this soup.

—

Peel the cucumbers and chop or grate them finely.

Beat the yoghurt with the iced water in a bowl until it is smooth and creamy. Add the cucumber, garlic and herbs and season with salt and pepper. Chill thoroughly before serving.

Serves 4

Chilled sour cherry soup

Meggyleves

450g (1lb) dark red sour cherries, preferably morello, pitted

225 ml (scant 1 cup) red wine

4 tablespoons sugar, or to taste

1 cinnamon stick

4–5 cloves

30g ($\frac{1}{4}$ cup) potato flour or cornflour (cornstarch)

225ml (1 cup) sour cream or smetana

Fruit soups are made all over Central and Eastern Europe – from cherries, apricots, plums, apples, rhubarb and all kinds of berries. Some are thickened with flour, others with eggs; either red or white wine may be used, depending on the colour of the fruit. Traditionally they are served at the beginning of the meal to whet the appetite, or after the main course to freshen the palate, like a sorbet. They also make a very good mid-afternoon snack. Fruit soups can be served hot or cold, with a dollop of sour cream, crème fraîche or strained yoghurt.

—

Place the cherries in a saucepan with the red wine, sugar, cinnamon and cloves. Pour in 1 litre (4 cups) water and bring to the boil, then simmer for 10 minutes or until the cherries are soft.

In a small bowl, mix the potato flour with a little cold water to make a smooth paste, then gradually stir in a couple of ladlefuls of the hot soup. Stir this mixture back into the soup and simmer, but do not boil, until the soup is thickened. Remove the cinnamon stick and cloves and chill thoroughly. Serve in individual bowls with sour cream on the side.

Serves 4

Ashkenazi beetroot soup
Borscht

450g (1lb) raw beetroots (beets)

3 tablespoons lemon juice,
or to taste

2–3 teaspoons sugar, to taste

3 egg yolks

salt and freshly ground black
pepper

boiled or mashed potatoes,
to serve

There are many variations of this classic Ashkenazi soup. Sometimes the eggs are omitted and the soup is served chilled, with a dollop of sour cream. Other cooks like to add a little grated onion or apple, but in this recipe the soup is thickened with egg yolks and served hot, with boiled or mashed potatoes.

—

Peel the beetroots and slice them thinly. Place in a large saucepan with 1 litre (4 cups) water and bring to the boil. Cover and simmer for 30 minutes or until the beetroots are tender and the liquid is dark red. Strain the soup, discarding the beetroots.

Return the soup to the pan and stir in the lemon juice and sugar. Beat the egg yolks in a bowl and gradually add a ladleful of hot soup. Pour the mixture back into the soup and mix well. Heat thoroughly, but do not let the soup boil or it will curdle. Season with salt and pepper, then serve hot with boiled or mashed potatoes.

Serves 3–4

Russian cabbage soup

Shchi

2 tablespoons butter

1 large onion, finely chopped

2 garlic cloves, finely chopped

1 green or white cabbage, about 450g (1lb), finely shredded

1 medium carrot, coarsely grated

2 medium 'floury' potatoes, peeled and diced

4 ripe plum tomatoes, peeled, deseeded and chopped

2 bay leaves

1 litre (4 cups) vegetable stock or water

salt and freshly ground black pepper

2 tablespoons finely chopped dill or parsley

sour cream or smetana, to serve

Shchi is one of the most famous soups in Russia. It is usually made with white or green cabbage, but some versions are made with other green leafy vegetables, especially spinach, sorrel or nettles. *Shchi* is usually served with sour cream or smetana and some black bread on the side.

—

Heat the butter in a large saucepan and add the onion and garlic. Cook over a moderate heat until the onion is translucent. Add the cabbage and carrot and continue to cook for a few minutes, stirring from time to time so the vegetables cook evenly. Add the potatoes, tomatoes, bay leaves and stock and bring to the boil. Season with salt and pepper, then cover and simmer for a further 20–25 minutes, adding a little water if the soup seems too thick. Serve hot in individual bowls, garnished with dill or parsley and a dollop of sour cream.

Serves 4

Cauliflower soup with sour cream and gruyère

Karfiol polievka

1 medium cauliflower, broken into florets

1 litre (4 cups) hot water

2 tablespoons butter

2 tablespoons flour

grating of nutmeg

salt and freshly ground black pepper

freshly grated gruyère cheese, sour cream and finely chopped parsley, to serve

This creamy cauliflower soup is very quick and easy to prepare. Sometimes a little grated gruyère cheese is stirred into the soup just before serving, which gives it a lovely flavour.

—

Place the cauliflower florets and the hot water in a large saucepan and bring to the boil. Cover and simmer for 15 minutes or until the cauliflower is tender. Force the soup through a sieve or puree in a blender.

Melt the butter in a small pan and stir in the flour. Cook over a moderate heat for 2–3 minutes without browning. Gradually add a ladleful of the hot soup, stirring constantly, so no lumps are formed. Pour this mixture back into the soup and mix well. Simmer for 10 minutes, adding a little more water if the soup is too thick. Season with nutmeg, salt and pepper, then simmer for 5 more minutes – don't let it boil. Stir in the grated cheese and serve the soup at once, garnished with a dollop of sour cream and a sprinkling of parsley.

Serves 4

Pied-Noir garlic soup

Soupe à l'ail

2 tablespoons extra virgin olive oil

8 garlic cloves, finely chopped

1 litre (4 cups) hot water

75g ($\frac{3}{4}$ cup) vermicelli

salt and freshly ground black pepper

2 egg yolks

50g ($\frac{1}{2}$ cup) grated gruyère cheese

The term Pied-Noir originally referred to French colonizers in Algeria in the nineteenth century, but later it was applied to anyone of French, Italian, Spanish or Portuguese origin (most of whom were Jewish) living in the Maghreb. A similar soup to this one, but without the vermicelli and cheese – called *sopa de maimonedes* – is made by the Jews of Andalusia.

—

Heat the olive oil in a large saucepan and cook the garlic over a moderate heat for 1–2 minutes without browning. Add the hot water and bring to the boil. Cover and simmer for 10 minutes, then bring back to the boil. When the soup is boiling, add the vermicelli and season with salt and pepper, then cook for a further 10 minutes or until the vermicelli is tender but still firm.

Beat the egg yolks in a small bowl and gradually add a ladleful of the hot soup, stirring constantly. Return to the pan and mix well. Heat thoroughly, but do not let the soup boil or it will curdle. Stir in the grated cheese and serve at once.

Serves 4

Tomato soup with potatoes and parsley

Sopa de tomate

2 tablespoons extra virgin olive oil

2 medium onions, chopped

1 carrot, coarsely grated

2 medium potatoes, peeled and diced

675g (1½lb) ripe plum tomatoes, peeled, deseeded and chopped

handful of finely chopped flat-leaf parsley, plus extra, to serve

1 litre (4 cups) vegetable stock or water

pinch of sugar

salt and freshly ground black pepper

This classic tomato soup has a lovely flavour and texture. Fresh tomatoes are best for this recipe.

—

Heat the olive oil in a large saucepan and cook the onions and carrot over a moderate heat for 5 minutes. Add the potatoes, tomatoes, parsley and stock and bring to the boil. Add the sugar and season with salt and pepper. Cover and simmer for 30 minutes, then force the soup through a sieve or puree in a blender.

Return the soup to the pan and heat thoroughly, adding a dash of hot water if it seems too thick. Serve hot, sprinkled with a little more parsley.

Serves 4–6

North African broad bean soup

Bessara

350g (2 cups) skinless split dried broad (fava) beans

4–5 garlic cloves, crushed

2 medium onions, chopped

40g (1½ cups) finely chopped flat-leaf parsley

1 teaspoon ground cumin

½ teaspoon paprika

¼ teaspoon cayenne pepper

salt

4 tablespoons extra virgin olive oil

Bessara or *bichra* (broad [fava] bean soup) is made by Jews all over North Africa. In Egypt, it usually includes a mixture of coriander (cilantro), parsley, dill, mint and dried melokhia – also called Jew's mallow, which can be found in most Middle Eastern grocers. Tunisian Jews usually add a little potato to the soup and spice it strongly with harissa. This recipe comes from Fez, in Morocco, where it is often served for Sukkot or during Passover. Skinless split dried broad (fava) beans are best for this recipe, and are widely available in Middle Eastern stores.

—

Soak the beans for 2 hours, then drain. Place in a large saucepan with the garlic, onions, parsley and 1 litre (4 cups) water and bring to the boil. Cover and simmer for 2 hours, or until the broad beans are tender. Force through a sieve or puree in a blender, then return the soup to the pan. The finished soup should be very thick, but add a little hot water if it seems too thick. Add the spices and season with salt. Simmer for a further 10 minutes to blend the flavours. Just before serving, stir in the olive oil.

Serves 4

Wild mushroom and barley soup

Krupnik

15g ($\frac{1}{2}$ cup) dried cep or porcini mushrooms

65g ($\frac{1}{3}$ cup) pearl barley

2 tablespoons butter

1 medium onion, chopped

1 carrot, diced

1 celery stalk, diced

2 medium potatoes, peeled and diced

75g ($\frac{1}{2}$ cup) green beans, trimmed and cut into 2cm ($\frac{3}{4}$in) lengths

1.25 litres (5 cups) vegetable stock

salt and freshly ground white pepper

2 tablespoons finely chopped flat-leaf parsley

sour cream or smetana, to serve (optional)

This classic winter soup is much loved by Jews from Lithuania, Poland and the Ukraine. Recipes range from a simple soup made with dried mushrooms, onions and barley, to a thicker vegetable soup, like this one from Lithuania that includes carrots, potatoes, celery and green beans. Across Eastern Europe, *krupnik* is often eaten during Sukkot, a holiday that usually coincides with the first frosts, so it's important to serve a soup that keeps you warm.

—

Soak the dried mushrooms in a little hot water for 30 minutes or until they are soft. Drain and reserve the soaking liquid. Chop the mushrooms coarsely.

Place the barley in a small bowl and cover with water. Leave to soak for 30 minutes, then drain.

Melt the butter in a large saucepan and cook the onion, carrot and celery over a moderate heat for 5 minutes. Add the mushrooms, barley, potatoes, green beans, stock and the reserved mushroom liquid and bring to the boil. Cover and simmer for 1–1$\frac{1}{2}$ hours or until the barley is soft and the soup is slightly thickened. Season with salt and pepper. Serve hot, garnished with parsley and a dollop of sour cream if desired.

Serves 4

White bean soup with tomatoes and chilli

Sopa de avikas

300g (1½ cups) dried gigantes, cannellini or butter (lima) beans

2 garlic cloves, finely chopped

l large onion, chopped

1 small red chilli, deseeded and finely chopped

250g (9oz) ripe tomatoes, peeled and chopped

½ teaspoon dried oregano

2 bay leaves

a large handful of flat-leaf parsley, finely chopped

4 tablespoons extra virgin olive oil

salt and freshly ground black pepper

lemon wedges, to serve

Similar to the well-known Greek *fassolada*, this soup was adopted by Jews all over Greece, who often served it for the Sabbath lunch, since it could be cooked very slowly overnight. This recipe comes from Thessaloniki, where they like to spike the soup with chilli. It is usually made with large white beans called gigantes. If they are unavailable, cannellini or butter (lima) beans may be used instead.

—

Soak the beans overnight, then drain.

Place the beans in a large saucepan with 1.25 litres (5 cups) water and bring to the boil. Add the garlic, onion, chilli, tomatoes, oregano, bay leaves and half of the parsley. Cover and simmer for 1½–2 hours or until the beans tender, adding a little hot water if the soup seems too thick. Add the remaining parsley and simmer for 5 more minutes. Just before serving, stir in the olive oil, season with salt and black pepper and serve hot, with lemon wedges on the side.

Serves 4

Iranian onion soup with fenugreek and mint

Eshkeneh

3 tablespoons butter or ghee

3 large onions, thinly sliced

2 tablespoons flour

1 teaspoon ground turmeric

1 teaspoon dried fenugreek

about 1 litre (4 cups) hot water

salt and freshly ground black pepper

2 eggs

3 tablespoons finely chopped mint

Said to date back to the third century BC, this soup was named after the Ashkanians, rulers of the Arsacid Empire that extended from Armenia to Afghanistan. Onions have long been thought to give men courage and strength, and it is believed this soup was a staple food of the Ashkanian warriors. Today it is enjoyed by Iranians and Jews alike, and is usually served with lavash or pita bread and lemon wedges or a drizzle of vinegar.

—

Melt the butter in a heavy saucepan, add the onions and cook over a gentle heat for 30–40 minutes or until they start to caramelize. Add the flour, turmeric and fenugreek, stirring constantly so no lumps are formed. Gradually pour in the hot water and bring to the boil. Season with salt and pepper, then simmer for 45 minutes.

Beat the eggs lightly in a bowl and gradually add a ladleful of hot soup, stirring constantly. Pour the egg mixture back into the soup and heat thoroughly – but do not let it boil or it will curdle. Serve hot, garnished with mint.

Serves 4

Pumpkin soup with yoghurt and chives

Sopa de balkabak

2 tablespoons extra virgin olive oil

1 medium onion, chopped

1 leek, white part only, thinly sliced

2 garlic cloves, finely chopped

900g (2lbs) pumpkin, peeled and diced

$\frac{1}{2}$ teaspoon ground cinnamon

$\frac{1}{2}$ teaspoon ground allspice

$\frac{1}{2}$ teaspoon sugar or to taste

salt and freshly ground black pepper

4 tablespoons yoghurt

2 tablespoons finely chopped chives

This classic pumpkin soup is traditionally made for the harvest festival of Sukkot. It is delicately flavoured with cinnamon and allspice and served with a dollop of thick creamy yoghurt and a sprinkling of chives.

—

Heat the olive oil in a large saucepan and cook the onion, leek and garlic over a moderate heat until softened. Add the pumpkin, spices, sugar and 1 litre (4 cups) water and bring to the boil. Cover and simmer for 30 minutes, then force the soup through a sieve or puree in a blender.

Return the soup to the pan and season with salt and pepper, then heat thoroughly, adding a little more water if the soup is too thick.

Serve in individual soup bowls, topped with a spoonful of yoghurt and a sprinkling of chives.

Serves 4

Ashkenazi split pea soup

Erbsensuppe

200g (1 cup) green split peas

4 tablespoons butter

1 medium onion, chopped

1 small leek, including the green part, thinly sliced

1 carrot, peeled and thinly sliced

1 medium potato, peeled and diced

1 parsnip, peeled and diced

1 litre (4 cups) hot water

salt and freshly ground black pepper

extra virgin olive oil, for drizzling

This warming winter soup is usually served with rye bread on the side.

—

Soak the split peas for 2 hours, then drain.

Melt half of the butter in a large saucepan and cook the onion and leek over a moderate heat until they are softened. Add the carrot, potato, parsnip, split peas and the hot water and bring to the boil. Cover and simmer for $1\frac{1}{2}$ hours or until the split peas are tender. Force the soup through a sieve or puree in a blender.

Return the soup to the pan and heat thoroughly, adding a little more water if the soup seems too thick. Stir in the remaining butter and season with salt and pepper. Serve hot, drizzled with olive oil.

Serves 4

Sorrel soup

Schav borscht

125g (4oz) sorrel leaves

450g (1lb) potatoes, peeled and diced

1 onion, chopped

1 litre (4 cups) vegetable stock or water

2 teaspoons sugar, or to taste

salt and freshly ground black pepper

125ml ($\frac{1}{2}$ cup) sour cream or smetana

This soup from Transylvania is made by Jews all over Eastern Europe, and is traditionally prepared for Shavuot. Some versions include beaten eggs, others are served with mashed potatoes on the side. If sorrel is unavailable, spinach or watercress and a tablespoon or two of lemon juice may be used instead, but it will not have quite the same tart flavour.

—

Wash the sorrel and remove any tough stalks. Chop coarsely.

Place the potatoes and onion in a large saucepan with the stock. Bring to the boil, then cover and simmer for 30 minutes. Add the sorrel and sugar and simmer for 5 more minutes, then season with salt and pepper. Mash the potatoes with a potato ricer or puree the soup in a blender or food processor.

Return the soup to the pan and heat thoroughly, adding a little water if the soup is too thick, then remove from the heat and stir in the sour cream. Serve hot or cold.

Serves 4

Algerian vegetable soup

Boketof

4 tablespoons extra virgin olive oil

2 medium onions, chopped

2 garlic cloves, finely chopped

3 courgettes (zucchini), trimmed and cut into small dice

250g (9oz) potatoes, peeled and cut into small dice

2 ripe tomatoes, peeled and chopped

1 bay leaf

1–2 teaspoons harissa (see page 36), to taste

1 teaspoon paprika

$\frac{1}{2}$ teaspoon ground coriander

1.25 litres (5 cups) hot water

1 tablespoon concentrated tomato puree (paste), dissolved in a little hot water

salt and freshly ground black pepper

100g (1 cup) spaghetti, broken into 2cm ($\frac{3}{4}$in) lengths

juice of 1 lemon, or to taste

2 tablespoons finely chopped mint leaves

2 tablespoons torn basil leaves

This soup is often served for the festival of Tisha Be-Av which is always celebrated with a dairy-free meal. Sometimes *boketof* is made with fresh or dried beans instead of potatoes.

—

Heat the olive oil in a large saucepan and cook the onions and garlic over a moderate heat for 2 minutes. Add the courgettes, potatoes, tomatoes and bay leaf, then stir in the harissa, paprika and coriander. Add the hot water and tomato puree and bring to the boil. Cover and simmer for 1 hour, then bring back to the boil. Season with salt and pepper. Add the spaghetti and cook for 10 minutes or until the spaghetti is tender but still firm. Just before serving, add the lemon juice, mint and basil. Serve hot.

Serves 4–5

Lentil and rice soup for Yom Kippur

Harira de Kippur

200g (1 cup) whole brown lentils

4 tablespoons butter or ghee

2 medium onions, chopped

2 garlic cloves, finely chopped

2 celery stalks with leaves, thinly sliced

1 teaspoon ground coriander

½ teaspoon ground turmeric

½ teaspoon saffron threads, dissolved in 2 tablespoons hot water

450g (1lb) ripe plum tomatoes, peeled and forced through a sieve or pureed in a food processor

1.25 litres (5 cups) hot water

75g (½ cup) long-grain rice or orzo – or vermicelli, broken into 2cm (¾in) lengths

salt and freshly ground black pepper

1½ tablespoons flour

juice of ½–1 lemon, to taste

2 tablespoons finely chopped flat-leaf parsley

2 tablespoons finely chopped coriander (cilantro)

This nourishing soup was originally a Bedouin dish that was adopted by Arab Muslims, and later by the Jews. Traditionally harira was served to break a fast, during Ramadan or for Yom Kippur, but today it is served throughout the year for breakfast, lunch or dinner. There are many variations of harira, but it is usually based on lentils or chickpeas (garbanzo beans), tomatoes, onion, garlic, herbs and spices, thickened with flour and delicately flavoured with lemon juice. Sometimes vermicelli or orzo – small pellets of pasta the size of a grain of rice – is used instead of rice.

—

Soak the lentils for 2 hours, then drain.

Melt the butter in a large saucepan and add the onions, garlic and celery. Cook over a moderate heat for 2–3 minutes. Stir in the ground coriander, turmeric, saffron liquid and tomatoes. Add the lentils and the hot water and bring to the boil, then cover and simmer for 1 hour or until the lentils are tender. Add the rice and season with salt and pepper. Simmer for a further 15 minutes or until the rice is tender but still firm.

Place the flour in a small bowl and mix with enough cold water to make a smooth paste. Add a few tablespoonfuls of the hot soup and mix well, then pour back into the pan and cook over a gentle heat for a further 10 minutes or until the flour is cooked and the soup is slightly thickened. Stir in the lemon juice and herbs and serve hot.

Serves 4–6

Sabbath minestrone

Minestrone del Sabato

3 tablespoons extra virgin olive oil

1 medium onion, chopped

2 garlic cloves, finely chopped

1 celery stalk, diced

1 teaspoon finely chopped oregano

1 carrot, diced

2 medium courgettes (zucchini), diced

1 medium potato, peeled and diced

100g ($\frac{2}{3}$ cup) cooked and drained cannellini beans

100g ($\frac{2}{3}$ cup) freshly shelled or frozen peas

400g (14oz) ripe plum tomatoes, peeled and chopped

250g (9oz) spinach, cut into 2cm ($\frac{3}{4}$in) strips

50g ($\frac{1}{2}$ cup) spaghetti or vermicelli, broken into 2cm ($\frac{3}{4}$in) lengths

salt and freshly ground black pepper

freshly grated pecorino or parmesan cheese

This classic minestrone soup comes from Rome's Jewish community. A good minestrone soup should be thick with vegetables, pasta or rice and never watery. The vegetables can vary according to the season – turnip, leek, cabbage, broad (fava) beans, Swiss chard, or beet greens are all possible additions.

—

Heat the olive oil in a large saucepan and cook the onion, garlic, celery and oregano over a moderate heat for 2 minutes. Add the carrot, courgettes, potato, cannellini beans, peas, tomatoes, spinach and 1 litre (4 cups) water and bring to the boil. Cover and simmer for 1$\frac{1}{2}$ hours, then add the spaghetti and season with salt and pepper. Cook for a further 15 minutes or until the spaghetti is tender but still firm. Serve hot, with grated cheese on the side.

Serves 4

Pasta and dumplings

'If there is food for three, there is food for four'

JUDEO-SPANISH PROVERB

The origins of pasta are unclear. *Itria* or *lagani* (strips of dough made with flour and water) were made by the ancient Greeks and Romans, but it is not known whether they were boiled in water like pasta. Arabic texts of the tenth century mention *itriyeh* (ribbons of dried dough), and later medieval manuscripts referred to ribbons of fresh pasta called *rishteh*, meaning 'strings'. Certainly Jews have been preparing pasta in the Rhineland since the fourteenth century, when it was probably introduced by Jewish merchants from Italy. Early names of pasta were *frimzeli*, *grimseli* and *vermesel*, all of which derive from the Italian vermicelli, whereas the Yiddish name *lokschen* derives from the Persian *lakhshah*. *Lokschen* is usually cut into long thin ribbons, but on occasion it can sometimes be grated into small pellets – in which case it is called *farfel*.

It is thought that dumplings most likely evolved in different peasant cuisines around the world, born out of the same need to extend the calorific value of a dish as economically as possible. Dumplings have long been a staple across Central and Eastern Europe. They can be plain or stuffed, sweet or savoury, and are usually made of bread, potatoes or grains. Ukrainian *pampushki*, a relative of Polish *kartoffel klischkes*, are usually made of a mixture of grated and mashed potatoes, stuffed with curd cheese and shallow fried. Italian Jews, of course, make a wide variety of gnocchi from potatoes, semolina or from a mixture of spinach and ricotta.

Alsatian egg noodles

Frimsels

4 tablespoons butter

salt and freshly ground black pepper

crème fraîche and grated gruyère cheese, to serve

For the pasta

250g (2 cups) unbleached plain (all-purpose) flour

3 large eggs

$\frac{1}{4}$ teaspoon salt

These noodles have been made in Alsace since the fourteenth century. They are usually boiled in water or milk and then just tossed in butter, but in this recipe the frimsels are served topped with a dollop of crème fraîche and grated gruyère.

—

To make the pasta, place the flour in a mound on a large wooden board or work surface and make a deep well in the centre. Drop in one egg at a time and add the salt. Gradually beat in the flour with a fork, then form into a soft ball. Knead well for 10 minutes or until the dough is smooth and elastic. Do not add too much flour or the dough will become hard to roll. If the dough seems too dry, add a teaspoon or so of water. Wrap the dough in a damp cloth and allow it to rest for 30 minutes.

For the noodles, divide the pasta dough into four. Keep three parts wrapped. With a long thin rolling pin, quickly roll out the other part of the dough, making quarter turns to form a circle. When the dough is very thin and even, allow it to dry for 15 minutes. This will prevent the dough from sticking. Cut into noodles 3mm ($\frac{1}{8}$in) wide. Arrange the ribbons of pasta on a cloth and leave to dry. Repeat with the remaining portions of dough.

Cook the noodles in plenty of lightly salted boiling water until tender but still firm. Drain and transfer to a serving dish. Dot with butter and season with salt and pepper. Toss lightly and serve at once, with crème fraîche and grated cheese.

Serves 4

Tagliatelle with artichokes

Tagliatelle con i carciofi

8–9 frozen artichoke bottoms, thawed

3 tablespoons extra virgin olive oil

3 tablespoons butter

2 garlic cloves, finely chopped

3 tablespoons finely chopped flat-leaf parsley

salt and freshly ground black pepper

freshly grated parmesan cheese, to serve

For the tagliatelle

250g (2 cups) Italian 00 flour

3 large eggs

$\frac{1}{4}$ teaspoon salt

Frozen artichoke bottoms make this sauce very quick and easy to prepare. Thinly sliced artichoke bottoms are simply fried in a mixture of extra virgin olive oil and butter, that is delicately flavoured with garlic and parsley. Try to use a good fruity extra virgin olive oil.

—

To make the tagliatelle, follow the method for the pasta on page 86. Roll the dough out very thinly and leave to dry for 15 minutes, then roll up and cut into ribbons 5mm ($\frac{1}{4}$in) wide.

For the sauce, slice the artichoke bottoms very thinly. Heat the olive oil and half of the butter in a large frying pan and add the garlic, parsley and artichoke bottoms. Stir well, so they are evenly coated in oil and butter. Season with salt and pepper. Cook over a gentle heat until the artichokes start to turn golden, then add 3–4 tablespoons water and simmer for a few more minutes.

Meanwhile, cook the tagliatelle in plenty of lightly salted boiling water until tender but still firm. Drain and transfer to a warmed serving bowl. Dot with the remaining butter. Pour over the sauce and serve at once, with grated parmesan on the side.

Serves 4

Saffron noodles with tomatoes and harissa

Reuchtas

3 tablespoons extra virgin olive
oil

1 medium onion, finely chopped

5–6 garlic cloves, finely chopped

$\frac{1}{2}$ teaspoon harissa (see page 36),
or to taste

675g (1$\frac{1}{2}$lb) ripe tomatoes, peeled
and chopped

salt

For the saffron noodles

250g (2 cups) fine semolina,
or half fine semolina and half
unbleached plain (all-purpose)
flour

$\frac{1}{2}$ teaspoon powdered saffron

2 large eggs

2 egg yolks

$\frac{1}{2}$ teaspoon salt

These golden noodles are usually made with fine semolina
instead of flour, but they can also be made with a combination
of both. Serve with freshly grated parmesan cheese on the side,
if you like.

—

For the saffron noodles, follow the method for the pasta on page
86, beating the saffron with the eggs and egg yolks before
mixing with the semolina. Roll the dough out very thinly and
leave to dry for 15 minutes, then roll up and cut into ribbons
1cm ($\frac{1}{2}$in) wide.

Heat the olive oil in a large frying pan, add the onion and cook
over a moderate heat until it has softened. Add the garlic and
harissa and cook for 2 more minutes, then add the tomatoes and
season with salt. Cook over a moderate heat for 10 minutes or
until thickened.

Cook the noodles in plenty of lightly salted boiling water until
tender but still firm. Drain and transfer to a warmed serving
bowl. Pour over the tomato sauce, toss lightly and serve at once.

Serves 4

Hungarian noodles with cabbage

Kaposztas koczka

600g (1¼lb) white cabbage

50g (3½ tablespoons) butter

2 teaspoons sugar

salt and freshly ground
black pepper

For the noodles

250g (2 cups) unbleached
plain (all-purpose) flour

3 large eggs

½ teaspoon salt

Hungarians use a different pasta for almost every pasta dish, and so *kaposztas koczka* is always made with square egg noodles. The exact proportions of noodles to cabbage can vary, but those in the know are convinced that the noodles should always dominate.

—

Grate the cabbage and salt it lightly. Place in a colander set over a bowl and leave to stand for 30 minutes.

To make the noodles, follow the method for the pasta on page 86. Roll the dough out very thinly and leave to dry for 15 minutes. Roll up and cut into noodles 2cm (¾in) wide, then cut the noodles into 2cm (¾in) squares.

Lightly squeeze the excess juice out of the cabbage. Melt the butter in a large frying pan. Add the sugar and allow it to caramelize. Stir in the cabbage and season with salt and plenty of pepper. Cover and cook over a moderate heat until it has softened and is starting to turn golden brown, stirring from time to time so it cooks evenly and does not stick to the pan.

Cook the noodles in plenty of lightly salted boiling water until tender but still firm. Drain well. Add to the cabbage and stir well, so the noodles are well coated with hot butter. Serve at once.

Serves 4

Egg noodles with poppy seeds

Kluski z makiem

3 tablespoons butter

65g ($\frac{1}{2}$ cup) poppy seeds

2–3 tablespoons sugar or honey

For the egg noodles

250g (2 cups) unbleached plain (all-purpose) flour

3 eggs

pinch of salt

This dish is very easy to prepare, and surprisingly delicious. The best poppy seeds are dark blue in colour and have a mild, nutty flavour. They are available in most health food stores and good delicatessens.

—

To make the egg noodles, follow the method for the pasta on page 86. Roll the dough out very thinly and leave to dry for 15 minutes. Roll up and cut into ribbons 1cm ($\frac{1}{2}$in) wide. Cook in plenty of lightly salted boiling water until tender but still firm. Drain and transfer to a warmed serving bowl. Dot with butter and add the poppy seeds and sugar. Toss lightly and serve at once.

Serves 4

Wholemeal spaghetti with leeks, peppers and cherry tomatoes

Bigoli in salsa saporita

3 tablespoons extra virgin olive oil

3 garlic cloves, finely chopped

2 leeks, white part only, trimmed and thinly sliced

2 red or green (bell) peppers, cored, deseeded and cut into strips

450g (1lb) very ripe cherry tomatoes, cut in half

75g ($\frac{1}{2}$ cup) black and green olives, pitted and sliced

8 torn basil leaves

salt and freshly ground black pepper

450g (1lb) wholemeal (whole wheat) or 100% durum wheat spaghetti

1–2 tablespoons butter, cut into pieces

freshly grated parmesan cheese, to serve

Only made in Venice and Mantua, *bigoli* is a spaghetti-like pasta made from wholemeal (whole wheat) flour, eggs, a little warm water and salt. Traditionally the pasta dough is not rolled, but forced through a press called a *bigolaro* and comes out the other end as long thick strands of hollow spaghetti. Commercial wholemeal spaghetti may be used instead or, if you prefer, you can use durum wheat spaghetti.

—

Heat the olive oil in a large frying pan and cook the garlic and leeks over a moderate heat until they start to turn golden. Add the peppers, cover and simmer for 20 minutes or until they are tender. Add the tomatoes and olives and cook for 5 more minutes. Add the basil and season with salt and pepper.

Meanwhile, cook the spaghetti in plenty of lightly salted boiling water until tender but still firm. Drain and transfer to a warmed serving bowl. Dot with butter and pour over the sauce. Serve at once, with grated parmesan on the side.

Serves 4

Egg noodles with lentils and caramelized onions

Rishta b' adas

200g (1 cup) brown lentils

4 tablespoons extra virgin olive oil

2 large onions, chopped

3–4 garlic cloves, crushed

handful of finely chopped flat-leaf parsley or coriander (cilantro), plus more to garnish

$\frac{1}{2}$ teaspoon ground cumin

$\frac{1}{2}$ teaspoon ground allspice

salt and freshly ground black pepper

225g (8oz) dried egg tagliatelle

Served with a leafy green salad on the side, this nourishing dish is perfect for a family dinner.

—

Soak the lentils for 2 hours and drain. Cook in boiling water for 45 minutes or until they are tender. Drain and set aside.

Heat the olive oil in a large frying pan and cook the onions over a moderate heat until browned. Add the garlic, spices and parsley and season with salt and pepper. Add the lentils and stir well. Simmer for 5 minutes to blend the flavours.

Cook the tagliatelle in plenty of lightly salted boiling water until it is tender but still firm. Drain well and add to the lentil sauce. Mix well and serve at once, garnished with parsley.

Serves 3–4

Jewish-style cold tagliolini

Tagliolini freddi alla ebraica

3 tablespoons extra virgin olive oil

2 garlic cloves

½ small red chilli, deseeded and finely chopped

handful of finely chopped flat-leaf parsley

2 tablespoons torn basil leaves

675g (1½lb) ripe plum tomatoes, peeled, deseeded and chopped

salt

2 tablespoons balsamic vinegar

For the tagliolini

250g (2 cups) Italian '00' flour

3 large eggs

¼ teaspoon salt

This classic Sabbath dish was often made by the Jewish communities of central Italy, especially in Ancona, where they like to spice their food with a little *peperoncino* or chilli. Traditionally it was prepared on Friday, left overnight to absorb the sauce and then served cold for lunch on Saturday – but you can, of course, serve it hot or warm too.

—

To make the tagliolini, follow the method for the pasta on page 86. Roll out the dough very thinly and leave to dry for 15 minutes, then roll up and cut into ribbons about 3mm (⅛in) wide.

Heat the olive oil in a large frying pan and cook the garlic and chilli for 1 minute. Add the parsley and basil and cook for a further 2 minutes. Add the tomatoes and season with salt. Cook over a moderate heat for 10 minutes or until the sauce starts to thicken. Add the vinegar and simmer for a few more minutes.

Meanwhile, cook the tagliolini in plenty of lightly salted water until tender but still firm. Drain and transfer to a serving bowl. Pour over the sauce and toss lightly. Set aside for 30 minutes so the pasta absorbs the sauce or chill overnight in the refrigerator and serve at room temperature.

Serves 4

Keskasoon pasta with chickpeas

Keskasoon

2 tablespoons extra virgin olive oil

1 large onion, finely chopped

2 garlic cloves, finely chopped

300g (10oz) keskasoon or acine di pepe pasta

150g ($\frac{3}{4}$ cup) cooked and drained chickpeas (garbanzo beans)

400ml ($1\frac{3}{4}$ cups) hot water

salt and freshly ground black pepper

2 tablespoons butter

The small round Syrian pasta called *keskasoon* resembles large-grain couscous, and is traditionally prepared for Rosh Hashanah (Jewish New Year). Round foods, such as peas, chickpeas, *keskasoon* or couscous, are served at this time as they symbolize fertility, prosperity and the ever-turning wheel of life. If *keskasoon* is unavailable, Italian *acine di pepe* pasta may be used instead. Like the Judeo–Spanish *fideos*, keskasoon are first browned in oil, before they are cooked in water like rice. This dish is also very good served with freshly grated parmesan on the side.

—

Heat the olive oil in a large frying pan and cook the onion over a moderate heat until it is softened and starting to turn golden. Add the garlic and continue to cook for 1–2 minutes without browning. Add the pasta and cook for a further 3–4 minutes or until it turns golden, stirring constantly to prevent it from sticking to the bottom of the pan. Add the chickpeas and the hot water and season with salt and pepper. Stir well, then cover and simmer for 20 minutes or until the pasta is tender and the water has been absorbed. Transfer to a serving dish and dot with butter. Serve at once.

Serves 4

Spinach and ricotta ravioli with basil and walnut pesto
Ravioli di spinaci e ricotta con pesto

2 tablespoons butter

freshly grated parmesan cheese, to serve

For the ravioli dough

250g (2 cups) Italian '00' flour

3 eggs

1 tablespoon extra virgin olive oil

pinch of salt

For the filling

450g (1lb) spinach

350g (1½ cups) ricotta cheese

1 egg, plus 1 yolk

50g (½ cup) freshly grated parmesan cheese

grating of nutmeg

salt and freshly ground black pepper

For the basil and walnut pesto

pinch of coarse sea salt

1–2 garlic cloves, peeled

1 tablespoon pine nuts

1 tablespoon freshly shelled walnuts, finely ground in a blender or food processor

30g (1oz) basil leaves

2 tablespoons freshly grated parmesan cheese

4 tablespoons extra virgin olive oil

These delicious ravioli are often served for Tu Bi-Shevat, the Festival of the Trees. They are also very good with a light tomato sauce or simply dressed with melted butter and freshly grated parmesan cheese.

—

To make the ravioli dough, follow the method for the pasta on page 86, adding the olive oil with the eggs.

While the pasta dough rests, make the filling. Wash the spinach, then cook in a covered saucepan over a moderate heat for 5–7 minutes or until tender – the water on the leaves will prevent scorching. Squeeze dry and chop finely. Force the ricotta through a sieve into a bowl. Add the egg yolks, parmesan and spinach and blend well. Season with nutmeg, salt and pepper.

Roll out the pasta into two very thin rectangles of equal size. Place teaspoonfuls of the filling over one sheet of the dough at regular intervals, about 5cm (2in) apart. Cover with the other sheet of dough and press well around each mound. Cut the ravioli into 5cm (2in) squares with a pastry or ravioli cutter. Space them apart on a lightly floured tray and dry for 15 minutes.

Now prepare the pesto. Place the sea salt, garlic, pine nuts and walnuts in a large mortar and crush with a pestle to make a smooth sauce. Add a small amount of basil leaves and grind them against the sides of the mortar until they break apart. Repeat with the remaining basil until all used up and you have a coarse paste. Add the parmesan, then slowly drizzle in the olive oil, stirring with the pestle, until the sauce is smooth and creamy.

Cook the ravioli in lightly salted boiling water for 5–6 minutes or until tender. Drain, dot with the butter and spoon over the pesto. Toss lightly and serve with parmesan on the side.

Serves 6

Cheese ravioli for Shavuot

Ravioli de Chavuot

50g (3½ tablespoons) butter, melted

freshly grated parmesan cheese, to serve

For the ravioli dough

250g (2 cups) Italian '00' flour

3 large eggs

½ teaspoon salt

For the filling

350g (1½ cups) ricotta cheese

1 egg, plus 1 egg yolk

1 tablespoon sugar

pinch of salt

When they are made for Shavuot, these ravioli are usually filled with a mixture of ricotta, eggs, grated cheese and a dash of sugar, then served with melted butter and grated cheese, but they are also delicious with tomato sauce or pesto.

—

To make the ravioli dough, follow the method for the pasta on page 86.

While the pasta dough rests, make the filling. Place the ricotta, egg and egg yolk, sugar and salt in a bowl and mix well.

Roll out the pasta into two very thin rectangles of equal size. Place teaspoonfuls of the filling over one sheet of the dough at regular intervals, about 4cm (1½in) apart. Cover with the other sheet of dough and press well around each mound. Cut the ravioli into 5cm (2in) squares with a pastry or ravioli cutter. Line them up on a lightly floured board or tray, making sure they do not touch, and leave for 15 minutes to dry.

Cook the ravioli in plenty of lightly salted boiling water for 5–6 minutes or until they float to the surface. Remove with a slotted spoon and transfer to a warmed serving dish. Pour over the melted butter and sprinkle with grated parmesan. Serve at once.

Serves 4

Pumpkin ravioli with butter and sage

Tortelli di zucca

4 tablespoons butter

5–6 sage leaves, coarsely chopped

freshly grated parmesan cheese, to serve

For the filling

1 small pumpkin, about 900g (2lb)

60g ($\frac{1}{2}$ cup) amaretti, crushed

about 100g (1 cup) freshly grated parmesan cheese

salt and freshly ground black pepper

For the ravioli dough

250g (2 cups) Italian '00' flour

3 large eggs

$\frac{1}{2}$ teaspoon salt

The filling for these ravioli is made simply with baked pumpkin, crushed amaretti, grated parmesan and lemon rind. The exact amount of grated cheese needed will depend on how much moisture remains in the baked pumpkin. Sometimes a couple of tablespoons of raisins are added to the filling.

—

To make the filling, bake the pumpkin in a preheated 200°C/ 400°F/gas 6 oven for 1 hour or until the pumpkin is very soft. Cut in half and remove the seeds. Scoop out the flesh. Drain well and squeeze out as much liquid as you can. Transfer the pumpkin flesh to a mixing bowl and add the amaretti and enough grated parmesan to hold the mixture together. Season with salt and pepper.

To make the ravioli dough, follow the method for the pasta on page 86. Roll out the pasta into two very thin rectangles of equal size. Place heaped teaspoonfuls of the filling over one sheet of the dough at regular intervals, about 4cm (1$\frac{1}{2}$in) apart. Cover with the other sheet of dough and press well around each mound. Cut the ravioli into 4cm (1$\frac{1}{2}$in) squares with a pastry or ravioli cutter. Line them up on a lightly floured board or tray, making sure they do not touch, and leave for 15 minutes to dry.

Cook the ravioli in plenty of lightly salted boiling water for 5–6 minutes or until tender.

Meanwhile, melt the butter in a small frying pan and add the sage. Let it sizzle for a few minutes or until the butter starts to turn golden brown.

Carefully remove the cooked ravioli with a slotted spoon, transfer to a warmed serving dish. Pour over the melted butter and sage and serve at once, with plenty of parmesan on the side.

Serves 4

Baked green lasagne with wild mushrooms

Lasagne verde al forno

250g (9oz) buffalo mozzarella or scamorza, diced

100g (1½ cups) freshly grated parmesan cheese

For the lasagne dough

125g (4oz) spinach leaves

250g (2 cups) Italian '00' flour

2 eggs

½ teaspoon salt

For the mushroom and tomato sauce

3 tablespoons extra virgin olive oil

2 garlic cloves, finely chopped

2 teaspoons finely chopped oregano

375g (13oz) fresh porcini or other mushrooms, thinly sliced

450g (1lb) ripe plum tomatoes, peeled, deseeded and chopped

In this dish from Ferrara, the lasagne is layered with a rich mushroom and tomato sauce, buffalo mozzarella, grated cheese and béchamel sauce. It is perfect for a dinner party or family meal.

—

To make the lasagne dough, wash the spinach thoroughly, then cook in a covered saucepan over a moderate heat for 5 minutes or until wilted – the water clinging to the leaves is sufficient to prevent scorching. Drain, squeeze dry and chop finely.

Place the flour in a mound on a large wooden board or work surface and make a deep well in the centre. Drop in the eggs, spinach and salt. Gradually beat in the flour with a fork, then form into a soft ball. Knead well for 8–10 minutes or until the dough is smooth and elastic. Do not add too much flour or the dough will become hard to roll. If the dough seems too dry, add a teaspoon or so of water. Wrap the dough in a damp cloth and allow it to rest for 30 minutes.

Roll the dough out fairly thinly and cut into rectangles about 18cm x 10cm (7in x 4in). Cook about six lasagne sheets at a time in plenty of lightly salted boiling water until tender but still firm. Remove with a slotted spoon and dip in a bowl of cold water, then lay out on a clean tea towel to dry. Repeat until all the lasagne sheets are cooked.

Meanwhile, heat the olive oil in a large frying pan and cook the garlic and oregano over a moderate heat for 2 minutes. Add the mushrooms and continue to cook until they are tender. Add the tomatoes, season well and cook, uncovered, for a further 10 minutes or until the sauce starts to thicken.

Continued over the page...

For the béchamel sauce

4 tablespoons butter

3 tablespoons plain (all-purpose) flour

450ml (2 cups) hot milk

grating of nutmeg

salt and freshly ground black pepper

To make the béchamel sauce, melt the butter in a heavy saucepan. Add the flour and cook for 1 minute without browning, stirring constantly. Pour in a little hot milk and stir vigorously with a wooden spoon until the mixture is free of lumps. Gradually add the rest of the hot milk, a little at a time, until it is all incorporated and the sauce is smooth and creamy. Season with nutmeg, salt and pepper and simmer for another minute or two.

Grease a large shallow baking dish and arrange a layer of lasagne over the bottom. Spoon over a layer of the tomato and mushroom sauce and cover with béchamel sauce. Dot with mozzarella and sprinkle grated parmesan over the top. Repeat the layers until all the ingredients are used up, ending with lasagne, béchamel sauce and parmesan. Bake in a preheated 180°C/350°F/gas 4 oven for 30–40 minutes or until the top is golden and the sauce is bubbling.

Serves 4

Green gnocchi
Gnocchi verde

4 tablespoons butter

5–6 sage leaves, roughly chopped

freshly grated parmesan cheese, to serve

For the gnocchi

900g (2lb) spinach

350g ($1\frac{1}{2}$ cups) ricotta, mashed with a fork

2 egg yolks

about 75g ($\frac{3}{4}$ cup) freshly grated parmesan cheese

grating of nutmeg

salt and freshly ground black pepper

flour, for dredging

These deliciously light dumplings are usually served simply with sage butter and a sprinkling of grated parmesan. They are also very good topped with melted butter or the sauce of your choice and grated cheese, then baked in the oven. Sometimes you might need to add a little more grated cheese or a tablespoon or two of flour if the mixture is too wet. To test, drop a dumpling into the boiling water – it should hold its shape without falling apart.

—

To make the gnocchi, wash the spinach thoroughly, then cook in a covered saucepan over a moderate heat for 5 minutes or until wilted – the water clinging to the leaves is sufficient to prevent scorching. Drain, squeeze dry and chop finely. Place in a mixing bowl with the ricotta, egg yolks and parmesan. Mix well and season with nutmeg, salt and pepper. If the mixture seems too soft, add a little more grated parmesan. Form into dumplings about the size of a walnut and dredge in flour to coat lightly.

Drop about half of the dumplings into a large pan of lightly salted boiling water and cook for 8–10 minutes – the dumplings will float to the surface when they are cooked.

Meanwhile, melt the butter in a small frying pan, add the sage leaves and simmer for about 30 seconds then remove the pan from the heat.

Using a slotted spoon, lift out half of the cooked gnocchi and transfer to a warmed serving bowl. Pour over half of the melted butter and sage, then sprinkle with grated parmesan. Repeat with the remaining gnocchi, piling them on the first batch and topping them with the remaining butter and sage and sprinkling with parmesan. Serve at once, with more parmesan on the side.

Serves 4

Potato dumplings stuffed with curd cheese and chives

Pampushki

450g (1lb) potatoes, peeled

625g (2½ cups) mashed potato

olive oil, for shallow-frying

For the filling

225g (8oz) curd (pot or farmer's) cheese

1 egg yolk

1–2 tablespoons finely chopped chives

salt and freshly ground black pepper

Pampushki can be fried or boiled, sweet or savoury. For sweet *pampushki*, simply omit the chives from the filling, add a tablespoon or two of sugar and the grated rind of a lemon, then serve lightly dusted with sugar. In Russia they generally fry *pampushki* in vegetable oil, but as I believe cooking with vegetable oils can be bad for your health, I prefer to use olive oil instead.

—

To make the filling, place the curd cheese, egg yolk and chives in a bowl and mix well. Season with salt and pepper.

Coarsely grate the potatoes, then squeeze out as much water as possible. Place in a bowl with the mashed potato, season with salt and pepper and mix well. Form the potato mixture into balls about the size of an egg. Punch a hole in the centre with your forefinger and fill with a teaspoonful of filling, then close up to seal the filling inside. Flatten slightly and shallow-fry until golden on both sides. Drain on paper towels and serve hot.

Serves 4

Grains

'Love tastes sweet, but only with bread'

YIDDISH PROVERB

The trinity of wheat, olive oil and wine formed the foundation of the diet of the Hebrews in ancient Israel. Bread and wine also play an important role in Jewish religious practices, since most Jewish holiday meals begin with a prayer involving bread and wine. Grains – whether wheat, barley, rice or couscous – have always been a staple food in Jewish households and are served at most meals.

RICE

Rice is thought to have originated in Southeast Asia about 8500 BC. It then spread through China and India, and from there it was brought to Persia by migrating Turkic tribes about two thousand years ago. Around the second or third century BC, rice was introduced to the Middle East, where it became an important export under Roman rule – although it never became part of the diet of ancient Rome or Greece. In the eighth century, the Moors introduced rice to Spain, where it was soon incorporated into Sephardic cuisine. About the same time the Moors introduced rice to Sicily, but it did not appear in the rest of Italy until the fifteenth century, when it was planted in the Po Valley in Lombardy. Today rice is preferred to wheat in many regions of northern Italy. Rice was slow to reach northern and eastern Europe, and never played an important role in Ashkenazi cooking.

There are many different varieties of rice. In India, basmati rice is highly prized for its thin elongated grains and nutty flavour. In Italy and Spain, round short-grain rice is preferred, as it is more suitable for risotto and paella. Rice can be prepared in a variety of ways: boiled, steamed or baked, or even cooked in a bag dipped in simmering soup – a popular method with Bukharan Jews. In Iran, rice is usually par-boiled then steamed with a little oil or ghee until a golden brown crust called a *tahdig* is formed. This rice dish is called a *chelou* – or, if vegetables or fruit are added at the second stage of cooking, a *polow*.

COUSCOUS

Couscous is a staple food in all the countries of the Maghreb, from Morocco to Libya. Originally a Berber dish, it was later adopted by Arabs and Jews alike. Traditionally, North African Jews make couscous for festivals and special occasions, as well as the Sabbath. In Morocco, they usually prepare couscous with seven vegetables for Rosh Hashanah, as the number seven is said to bring good luck.

Couscous (called *seksu* by the Berbers, and *kuskusu* in Arabic) is a kind of grain-like pasta 1–2mm (about $\frac{1}{16}$in) in diameter, and usually made from semolina and flour. Larger granules of 3mm ($\frac{1}{8}$in) or more are called *berkoukes* or *mhamsa*. Unlike pasta, couscous is not kneaded into a dough, but laboriously rolled by hand into individual grain-like pellets. Fortunately, today it is manufactured commercially. Most of the packaged couscous available is pre-cooked, making it very quick and easy to prepare – simply follow the directions on the packet.

CORNMEAL

Corn or maize was first introduced to Europe in the sixteenth century, after the discovery of the New World. It was originally brought to Venice, where it soon became a staple of the poor, and was then taken to Constantinople. Although it never became an important food in Turkey, the Turks introduced it to Romania and Georgia, where it is still a staple today.

In Italy, cornmeal or polenta is usually made into a porridge and served with butter and grated cheese. When it cools, it sets firm and can then be sliced and fried or grilled, or made into pies layered with cheese and sauces.

In Romania, cornmeal porridge (*mamaliga*) is often topped with butter and sour cream or sheep's cheese, but is also made into a variety of pies and fritters.

BULGUR

Bulgur (or *burghul*, as it is called in Arabic) has been a staple food in the Middle East for thousands of years. Bulgur should not be confused with cracked wheat, which is simply raw crushed wheat grains, whereas bulgur is wheat that has been boiled, drained and dried before being milled into fine, medium or coarse grades. Fine bulgur is ideal for salads such as tabbouleh, while medium and coarse bulgur is used for pilafs, soups, stews and stuffings

KASHA

Buckwheat is not strictly a grain, but a plant of the same family as rhubarb and sorrel, whose seeds resemble a grain. Originating in Siberia and East Asia, it was brought to Eastern Europe in the Middle Ages. In Russia any grain – corn, barley, millet or rice – may be called kasha, but for Russian and Eastern European Jews kasha is always buckwheat. Traditionally, Ashkenazi Jews cook it in two ways – either as a porridge or with pasta 'bowties' (*kasha varnishkes*).

Spanish rice

Riz a l'espagnol

300g (1½ cups) long-grain rice

3 tablespoons extra virgin olive oil

2 garlic cloves, finely chopped

1 small onion, chopped

2 tablespoons flat-leaf parsley, finely chopped

2 frozen artichoke bottoms, thawed and thinly sliced

1 green (bell) pepper, cored, deseeded and cut into strips

2 red (bell) peppers, cored, deseeded and cut into strips

2 tomatoes, peeled and chopped

225g (½lb) freshly shelled or frozen peas

1 bay leaf

good pinch of cloves

salt and freshly ground black pepper

500ml (2½ cups) hot water

½ teaspoon powdered saffron, dissolved in 2 tablespoons hot water

This rice pilaf from North Africa is delicately flavoured with saffron and cloves. The choice of vegetables depends on the season: fennel, celery, green beans, diced carrots or baby broad (fava) beans all make good additions.

—

Wash the rice under cold running water and drain. Heat the olive oil in a heavy saucepan and cook the garlic, onion and parsley for 2 minutes. Add the artichoke bottoms and peppers and cook over a gentle heat for 10 minutes. Add the rice, tomatoes, peas, bay leaf and cloves and season with salt and pepper. Pour in the hot water and the saffron liquid and bring to the boil. Cover and simmer for 18–20 minutes or until the rice is tender, and small craters have appeared in the surface of the rice. Serve hot.

Serves 4

Bulgur pilaf with tomatoes and pine nuts

Burghul bi-banadoora

3 tablespoons extra virgin
olive oil or ghee

2 medium red onions, chopped

2 garlic cloves, finely chopped

3 tablespoons pine nuts

4 ripe tomatoes, peeled and
chopped

175g (1 cup) coarse bulgur

pinch of ground allspice

pinch of ground cinnamon

pinch of ground coriander

salt and freshly ground black
pepper

350ml (1½ cups) hot vegetable
stock or water

This dish is enjoyed by Muslims and Jews alike. The pine nuts add delicious flavour and texture.

—

Heat the olive oil in a heavy saucepan and cook the onions, garlic and pine nuts over a moderate heat until the onions are translucent. Add the tomatoes and continue to cook over a moderate heat for 7 minutes or until the sauce starts to thicken. Add the bulgur and spices and season with salt and pepper. Stir well, then simmer for 2 minutes. Pour in the hot stock and bring to the boil. Cover and simmer for 15 minutes or until the bulgur is tender and the liquid has evaporated. Remove from the heat and set aside for 5 minutes. Serve hot.

Serves 4

Rice with spinach and sumac

Rizz b'spanegh

3 tablespoons extra virgin olive oil

1 medium onion, finely chopped

4 garlic cloves, crushed

$\frac{1}{2}$ teaspoon ground coriander

$\frac{1}{4}$ teaspoon allspice

pinch of dried chilli flakes

450g (1lb) spinach, finely shredded

200g (1 cup) long-grain rice

325ml ($1\frac{1}{4}$ cups) hot water

1–2 teaspoons sumac, to taste

salt and freshly ground black pepper

This dish is a vibrant green colour. The exact proportion of spinach to rice varies widely: some recipes use as much as a kilo ($2\frac{1}{4}$lb) of spinach, others as little as 25g (1oz) of rice. Sumac is widely used in Middle Eastern cooking. It has a beautiful, deep red colour and tangy, lemony flavour and is mainly sprinkled over finished dishes, especially vegetables and salads, or added to dressings.

—

Heat the olive oil in a large heavy saucepan and add the onion. Cook over a moderate heat until it starts to turn golden. Add the garlic and spices and cook for another minute. Add the spinach and continue to cook for 10 minutes or until it is tender and the liquid has evaporated. Add the rice and the hot water and bring to the boil. Season with the sumac and salt and pepper, then cover and simmer for 18–20 minutes or until the rice is tender but still firm. Remove from the heat and set aside for 5 minutes. Serve hot, with extra sumac sprinkled on top.

Serves 4

Sephardic rice, chickpeas, tomatoes and oregano

Arroz asopado

300g (1½ cups) long-grain rice

4 tablespoons extra virgin olive oil

2 large onions, chopped

½ teaspoon dried oregano

175g (1¼ cups) cooked and drained chickpeas (garbanzo beans)

2 tomatoes, peeled and chopped

500ml (2 cups) hot water

salt and freshly ground black pepper

This dish from the island of Rhodes is often prepared as part of a dairy meal. If you like, you can serve it with some freshly grated kefalotyri or parmesan cheese on the side.

—

Wash the rice under cold running water and drain.

Heat the olive oil in a heavy saucepan and add the onions and oregano. Cook over a moderate heat for 8–10 minutes or until the onions start to turn golden. Add the rice and stir well, so that each grain is well coated in oil. Add the chickpeas, tomatoes and the hot water and season with salt and pepper. Bring to the boil, then cover and simmer for 18–20 minutes or until the water is absorbed and small craters appear in the surface of the rice. Serve hot.

Serves 4

Risotto with eight herbs

Risotto alle otto erbe

1 litre (4 cups) vegetable stock or water

2 tablespoons extra virgin olive oil

2–3 garlic cloves, finely chopped

large handful of finely chopped flat-leaf parsley

4 tablespoons torn basil leaves,

3 tablespoons finely chopped fennel fronds

2 tablespoons finely chopped chives

3–4 sage leaves, finely chopped

1–2 sprigs of rosemary, leaves picked and finely chopped

1–2 sprigs of thyme, leaves picked

300g (1½ cups) arborio rice

100ml (½ cup) dry white wine

salt and freshly ground black pepper

2 tablespoons unsalted butter

75g (¾ cup) freshly grated parmesan cheese

This recipe comes from Ancona, where the eight herbs used are basil, parsley, sage, thyme, rosemary, chives, wild fennel and garlic, but spring onions (scallions), shallots, oregano, marjoram, tarragon, celery leaves or borage can all be added.

—

Bring the stock to the boil in a saucepan and keep just below the simmering point.

Heat the olive oil in a heavy saucepan and cook the garlic and herbs over a moderate heat for 5 minutes. Add the rice and stir well, so that each grain is well coated in oil. Pour in the wine and season with salt and black pepper. Cook, stirring constantly, until the liquid has almost evaporated. Add a ladleful of stock and repeat until the rice is tender but still firm – the finished risotto should be creamy. Remove from the heat and stir in the butter and 3 tablespoons of the parmesan cheese. Serve at once, with the remaining cheese on the side.

Serves 4

Saffron rice with raisins and pine nuts

Arroz con pinones

300g (1½ cups) long-grain rice

3 tablespoons extra virgin olive oil

2 medium onions, chopped

75g (½ cup) pine nuts

3 tablespoons raisins

500ml (2 cups) hot vegetable stock or water

¼ teaspoon saffron threads, dissolved in 2 tablespoons hot water

salt and freshly ground black pepper

This saffron rice is often served for Rosh Hashanah (Jewish New Year), as the addition of raisins is said to sweeten the year ahead.

—

Wash the rice under cold running water and drain. Heat the olive oil in a heavy saucepan and cook the onions and pine nuts over a moderate heat until the onions are translucent. Add the rice and raisins and stir well, so each grain of rice is coated in oil. Add the hot stock and the saffron liquid and season with salt and pepper. Cover and simmer for 18–20 minutes or until the rice is tender but still firm, and small craters have appeared in the surface of the rice. Serve hot.

Serves 4

Lentils and rice with caramelized onions

Mujaddara

200g (1 cup) brown lentils

1 medium red onion, peeled and chopped

6 tablespoons extra virgin olive oil

200g (1 cup) long-grain rice

½ teaspoon ground allspice

½ teaspoon ground coriander

salt and freshly ground black pepper

2 large onions, sliced

This dish is said to come from the 'mess of pottage' for which Esau sold his birthright to his brother Jacob. The exact proportion of lentils to rice can vary from cook to cook, but the dish is always topped with a generous serving of fried onions. Sometimes a bowl of yoghurt is served on the side.

—

Soak the lentils for 2 hours, then drain. Place the lentils and 675ml (3 cups) water in a heavy saucepan and bring to the boil. Cover and simmer for 30 minutes or until they are almost tender. Drain, reserving the cooking liquid, then set aside.

Fry the chopped red onion in 2 tablespoons of the olive oil until it starts to turn golden brown. Add the rice, allspice and coriander and stir well, so the rice is well coated in oil. Add the lentils and the cooking liquid, mixed with enough hot water to make 450ml (2 cups) of liquid and bring to the boil. Season with salt and black pepper. Cover and simmer for a further 20 minutes or until the rice and lentils are tender and the liquid has been absorbed.

Meanwhile, heat the remaining 4 tablespoons of olive oil in a frying pan and cook the sliced onions over a moderate heat until they are a rich dark brown.

Serve the lentils and rice hot or warm, garnished with the fried onions.

Serves 4

Rice with prunes and cinnamon

Reizfloimes

300g (1½ cups) long-grain rice

2 tablespoons butter

2–3 shallots, finely chopped

125g (1 cup) pitted prunes, cut into quarters

75g (½ cup) raisins

1 teaspoon sugar

1 teaspoon ground cinnamon

500ml (2 cups) hot water

salt and freshly ground black pepper

This dish from Alsace is often served as a side dish for Friday night dinner.

—

Wash the rice under cold running water and drain. Melt the butter in a heavy saucepan, add the shallots and cook over a moderate heat until softened. Add the prunes and raisins and simmer for 2 minutes. Add the rice, sugar and cinnamon and stir well, so that each grain is well coated. Pour in the hot water and bring to the boil. Season with salt and pepper, then cover and simmer for 18–20 minutes or until the water is absorbed and small craters appear in the surface of the rice. Serve hot.

Serves 4

Couscous with butter and broad beans

Couscous au beurre

250g (1 ½ cups) freshly shelled or frozen baby broad (fava) beans

4 tablespoons butter

2–3 shallots, finely chopped

350g (2 cups) couscous

450ml (2 cups) hot water

salt and freshly ground black pepper

1 tablespoon icing (confectioners') sugar

1 teaspoon ground cinnamon

30g (¼ cup) raisins, soaked in hot water for 20 minutes

30g (¼ cup) blanched almonds, lightly toasted in a 180°C/350°F/gas 4 oven until golden

buttermilk or yoghurt, to serve

This dish is usually served for the festival of Mimouna, which is held at the end of Passover to mark the beginning of spring and the start of a new cycle of existence. At one time the festival was unique to the Jews of the Maghreb, but it is now also celebrated in Israel. The festive table is decorated with flowers and herbs, green ears of corn and barley and all kinds of pastries and confectionery, especially *jabane* (nougat), a raisin and walnut jam called *mrozya*, and *mofletah* (pancakes), usually served with mint tea. Like this couscous, the foods on the table are sweet; nothing is salted, nor is any black food or meat served. In the centre of the table is a plate of white flour topped with five broad (fava) bean pods filled with five eggs, five dates and five pieces of gold or silver – to invoke a prosperous year ahead. The display is not only intended to attract divine protection, but also to avert the evil eye.

—

Steam the broad beans for 15–20 minutes or until they are tender.

Meanwhile, melt half of the butter in a heavy saucepan and cook the shallots over a moderate heat until they are starting to turn golden. Add the couscous and stir well. Pour in the hot water and season with salt and pepper. Remove from the heat, cover with a tight-fitting lid and let stand for 5–10 minutes. Dot with the remaining butter and fluff up with a fork. Transfer to a warmed serving dish and shape into a mound. Dust with icing sugar and cinnamon and arrange the broad beans over the top. Scatter with raisins and almonds and serve at once, with a bowl of buttermilk or yoghurt on the side.

Serves 4

Rice with broad beans, tomatoes and dill

Timman ab baquili

3 tablespoons extra virgin olive oil or ghee

1 medium onion, finely chopped

$\frac{1}{2}$ teaspoon ground turmeric

$\frac{1}{4}$ teaspoon Aleppo pepper or smoked paprika

250g (2 cups) freshly shelled or thawed frozen baby broad (fava) beans

2 canned plum tomatoes, forced through a sieve or pureed in a food processor

500ml (2 cups) hot water

salt

300g (1$\frac{1}{2}$ cups) long-grain rice

handful of finely chopped dill

2 tablespoons finely chopped flat-leaf parsley

This dish has a lovely colour and flavour. It may be served hot or at room temperature with perhaps a dollop of yoghurt on the side.

—

Heat the olive oil in a heavy saucepan, add the onion and cook over a moderate heat until it starts to turn golden. Add the spices and cook for another minute. Add the broad beans, tomato puree and about 3 tablespoons of the hot water. Cover and simmer for 10–15 minutes or until the beans are almost tender. Season with salt. Add the rice, dill and the remaining hot water and bring to the boil. Cover and simmer for 18–20 minutes or until the rice is tender but still firm. Remove from the heat and set aside for 5 minutes. Serve hot, garnished with parsley.

Serves 4

Couscous with seven vegetables

Kesksou bil khodra

2 tablespoons extra virgin olive oil

2 medium onions, chopped

2 garlic cloves, crushed

1 tablespoon freshly grated ginger

1 teaspoon paprika

1 teaspoon ground cumin

½ teaspoon ground turmeric

4 ripe plum tomatoes, peeled, deseeded and cut into quarters

2 carrots, cut in half and then into 5cm (2in) lengths

2 turnips, cut into pieces roughly the same size as the carrots

1 small fennel bulb, trimmed and cut into wedges

200g (1 cup) cooked and drained chickpeas (garbanzo beans)

handful of finely chopped flat-leaf parsley

450g (1lb) courgettes (zucchini), halved lengthwise and cut into 5cm (2in) chunks

250g (9oz) butternut squash, cut into 5cm (2in) chunks

For the couscous

2 tablespoons butter

2 shallots, finely chopped

½ teaspoon ground cinnamon

350g (2 cups) couscous

450ml (2 cups) hot vegetable stock or water

salt and freshly ground black pepper

Seven vegetables are generally used for this recipe, as the number seven is said to bring good luck. For special occasions, such as Rosh Hashanah, it is often garnished with raisins and toasted almonds, but it is also very good topped with strips of sweet or hot peppers that have been fried in olive oil – these add a lovely touch of colour and flavour.

—

Heat the olive oil in a large saucepan and cook the onions over a moderate heat until softened. Add the garlic, ginger, paprika, cumin and turmeric and simmer for 2 minutes. Add the tomatoes, carrots, turnips, fennel, chickpeas, parsley and 450ml (2 cups) water and bring to the boil. Cover and simmer for 10 minutes. Add the courgettes and butternut squash and cook for a further 10–15 minutes or until the vegetables are tender but still hold their shape.

About 10 minutes before the end of cooking, start to prepare the couscous. Melt the butter in another saucepan and cook the shallots over a moderate heat until softened. Add the cinnamon and couscous and stir well. Pour in the hot stock and season with salt and pepper. Cover with a tight-fitting lid and leave to stand for 5–10 minutes. Fluff up with a fork and pile onto a warmed serving dish. Shape into a mound. Remove the vegetables from the stew and arrange over the couscous. Serve at once, with the soupy sauce on the side.

Serves 4

Venetian polenta pie

Polenta pasticciata

2 teaspoons salt

250g (1½ cups) polenta
(cornmeal)

750ml (3 cups) tomato sauce
(see page 137)

225g (8oz) fontina cheese,
thinly sliced

100g (1 cup) freshly grated
parmesan or grana padano
cheese

In this recipe from the Veneto, slices of polenta are layered
with tomato sauce, fontina and parmesan cheese, and baked
in the oven until golden. If you like, you can use buffalo
mozzarella instead of the fontina. A similar dish is made
for Shavuot with white polenta and béchamel instead of
tomato sauce.

—

Bring 1.25 litres (5 cups) water to the boil in a large heavy
saucepan. Add the salt and reduce the heat to a simmer. Slowly
pour in the polenta in a very thin, steady stream, stirring
constantly to prevent any lumps forming. Continue stirring until
the polenta starts to come away from the sides of the pan and has
lost any slight bitter taste – this can take 40–45 minutes. Spread
it thinly over a wooden board or baking sheet and leave to cool
and set.

When the polenta is cold, cut it into thin slices. Arrange a layer
of polenta over the bottom of a well-buttered baking dish and
cover with a layer of tomato sauce. Top with slices of fontina
and sprinkle with grated cheese. Repeat the layers until all the
ingredients are used up, ending with grated cheese.

Bake in a preheated 190°C/375°F/gas 5 oven for 30 minutes or
until the top is golden and the sauce is bubbling. Serve hot.

Serves 4–6

Romanian polenta with white cheese and sour cream

Mamaliga cu branza si smatana

1 teaspoon salt

250g (1½ cups) coarse polenta (cornmeal)

4 tablespoons butter

about 225g (8oz) crumbled feta or telemea (Romanian sheep's cheese)

sour cream, to serve

Polenta is a staple food in Romania, where it is often eaten as a porridge (*mamaliga*). Alternatively it may be spread out on a work surface and left to cool and set, so it can be sliced and used to make pies or fritters. *Mamaliga* is sometimes made with milk or a mixture of milk and water, which gives it a more creamy texture. Here it is served with sour cream and telemea, a tangy semi-soft white cheese made from sheep's milk – feta makes a good substitute.

—

Bring 1.25 litres (5 cups) water to the boil in a large heavy saucepan. Add the salt and reduce the heat to a simmer. Slowly pour in the polenta in a very thin, steady stream, stirring constantly to prevent any lumps forming. Continue stirring until the polenta starts to come away from the sides of the pan and has lost any slight bitter taste – this can take 40-45 minutes. You may need to add a little more hot water if the polenta gets too thick. Add the butter and sprinkle over the cheese. Serve at once with sour cream on the side.

Serves 4–6

Kasha with mushrooms

Kasha mit schveml

180g (1 cup) kasha (roasted buckwheat groats)

1 egg, lightly beaten

450ml (2 cups) hot water

grating of nutmeg

salt and freshly ground black pepper

3 tablespoons butter

2 medium onions, thinly sliced

250g (9oz) small white (button) mushrooms, thinly sliced

sour cream or smetana, to serve

Kasha, or roasted buckwheat, is a favourite food of Ashkenazi Jews from Poland and Russia. It has a delicious nutty flavour and is a very good source of protein, iron and calcium. Kasha is often cooked with beaten egg, which is said to help separate the grains. If you add 200g (7oz) pasta bow-ties or wide egg noodles broken into 2.5cm (1in) lengths, that have been cooked separately in lightly salted boiling water, then this dish becomes the well-known *kasha varnishkes* – often served by Eastern European Jews for Chanukah and Purim.

—

Place the kasha in a heavy saucepan and add the beaten egg. Stir well, so each grain is well coated, then cook over a gentle heat for 5 minutes or until the egg is set. Pour in the hot water and season with nutmeg, salt and pepper. Cover and simmer for 15 minutes, or until the kasha is tender and the liquid has been absorbed.

Meanwhile, melt the butter in a large frying pan and add the onions. Cook over a gentle heat until they start to turn golden. Add the mushrooms and continue to cook until they are tender and any liquid has evaporated. Stir the onions and mushrooms into the cooked kasha and simmer for 1–2 minutes.

Serve at once, with sour cream on the side.

Serves 4

Main courses

'He who eats slowly,
lengthens the days of his life'

JUDEO-SPANISH PROVERB

There are an enormous number of vegetarian dishes in the
Jewish kitchen, primarily because of the strict dietary laws that
forbid the combining of milk and meat products.

Every Jewish community has a variety of savoury pastries in
their culinary repertoire – from Sephardic *pastels*, *bulemas*,
filas and *tapadas*, Central European strudels and Middle Eastern
sambusaks to the Russian *piroshki*. These pastries are traditionally
served for festivals, weddings, bar mitzvahs and other special
occasions, as well as for *desayanu* – breakfast on the Sabbath.

The Sephardic Jews of Greece and Turkey are particularly noted
for their great love of vegetable dishes – especially gratins (called
almodrotes, *antchusas* and *esfongos*) and croquettes (*albondigas*,
fritikas and *keftes*). Syrian Jews make a variety of delicious
vegetarian dishes, including vegetables baked with eggs and
cheese (*b'jibn*), as well as stuffed vegetables (*mahshi*) dressed
with exotic sauces flavoured with tamarind or pomegranate syrup.

Ashkenazi Jews, on the other hand, have a more modest
vegetarian repertoire, due to the cooler climate of Northern
and Eastern Europe, which limits the availability of seasonal
vegetables. Nevertheless, they are great lovers of cabbage, carrots
and potatoes – which they use to make a variety of *kugels*
(puddings) and pancakes.

Artichoke tart

Torta di carciofi

1 tablespoon extra virgin olive oil

1 tablespoon butter

1 garlic clove, finely chopped

3 tablespoons finely chopped flat-leaf parsley

9–10 artichoke hearts in oil, drained

225ml (1 cup) double (heavy) cream, or half cream, half milk

1 egg, 2 egg yolks

25g ($\frac{1}{4}$ cup) grated emmenthal cheese

50g ($\frac{1}{2}$ cup) freshly grated parmesan cheese

grating of nutmeg

salt and freshly ground black pepper

For the pastry

100g ($\frac{3}{4}$ cup) plain (all-purpose) flour

65g ($\frac{1}{2}$ cup) wholemeal (whole wheat) flour

pinch of salt

75g ($\frac{1}{3}$ cup) butter

2 tablespoons iced water

This tart from Venice is filled with a delicious mixture of artichokes, cheese, eggs, parsley, a hint of garlic and cream. In Venice it is usually made with fresh artichoke hearts, but canned ones make it much quicker and easier.

—

To make the pastry, sift both the flours and salt into a bowl. Rub in the butter with your fingertips until the mixture resembles coarse breadcrumbs. Sprinkle over the iced water and form the dough into a soft ball, then wrap in foil and refrigerate for 1 hour.

Place the dough on a floured board and knead it briefly. Roll out into a circle about 30cm (12in) in diameter and 3mm ($\frac{1}{8}$in) thick. Roll the dough around the rolling pin and unroll it over a well-buttered 20cm (8in) tart tin. Ease the pastry into the corners, then trim any excess dough and crimp the edges with a fork. Prick the bottom in a few places. Cover the dough with foil and fill with baking beans to prevent the tart case from puffing up in the oven. Bake in a preheated 200°C/400°F/gas 6 oven for 8–10 minutes. When ready, the pastry should have shrunk away from the side of the tin. Remove from the oven and lift out the foil and beans. Turn the oven down to 180°C/350°F/gas 4.

Heat the olive oil and butter in a large frying pan and add the garlic and parsley. Cook over a moderate heat for 2 minutes, then add the artichoke hearts and cook over a gentle heat to blend the flavours. Set aside to cool slightly.

Beat the cream, egg and egg yolks together in a bowl, then stir in the emmenthal and half of the parmesan. Season with nutmeg, salt and pepper. Arrange the artichoke heart mixture in the tart case, then pour the egg mixture over the top. Sprinkle over the remaining parmesan and bake for 30 minutes or until the top is golden. Serve hot.

Serves 4

Sephardic aubergine coils

Bulemas de berendjena

2 medium aubergines
(eggplants), about 675g (1½lb)

1 tablespoon extra virgin olive oil

100g (½ cup) feta or beyaz peynir
(Turkish white cheese), mashed
with a fork

50g (½ cup) freshly grated
parmesan or kachkaval cheese

grating of nutmeg

freshly ground black pepper

8 large sheets fresh or thawed
frozen filo pastry

melted butter, for brushing

olive oil, for deep-frying

These delicious pastries are stuffed with a mixture of roasted
aubergines (eggplants), olive oil, feta and cheese then deep-
fried in olive oil. They are perfect for a snack, light lunch or
supper. Traditionally they are made for festivals and special
occasions, as well as for *desayanu* – a Sabbath breakfast
prepared by the Sephardim. *Bulemas* can also be brushed
lightly with olive oil and baked in the oven.

—

To make the filling, roast the aubergines in a preheated
200°C/400°F/gas 6 oven for 30 minutes or until they are soft
and the skins are blackened all over, turning them once or twice
so they cook evenly. When cool enough to handle, scoop out
the flesh and place in a colander to drain off any bitter juices.
Transfer to a bowl and mash with a fork. Stir in the olive oil, feta
and parmesan and mix well. Season with nutmeg and pepper.

Cut the filo pastry into rectangles about 30cm x 23cm (12in x
9in) and stack them in a pile. Lay a sheet of filo pastry on a clean
cloth, with the longer side facing you, and brush lightly with
melted butter. Repeat with a second sheet of filo pastry. Place a
thin line of filling about 2cm (¾in) thick along the longer side
of the pastry, about 2cm (¾in) from the edge. Fold over the edge
and roll up to make a long thin log, then roll up like a coiled
snake. Dip your fingertips in cold water and pinch the ends of
the coil to seal in the filling. Repeat with the remaining pastry
and filling.

Working in batches, deep-fry the bulemas in hot oil until crisp
and golden on both sides. Serve hot.

Serves 4

Aubergine, tomato and fontina pie

Pasticcio di melanzane

3 large aubergines (eggplants), about 1kg (2¼ lb)

salt

olive oil, for frying

2 eggs

1 tablespoon flour

50g (½ cup) freshly grated parmesan cheese

225ml (scant 1 cup) milk

200g (7oz) fontina cheese, thinly sliced

For the tomato sauce

2 tablespoons olive oil

2 garlic cloves, finely chopped

2 teaspoons finely chopped oregano

675g (1½lb) ripe plum tomatoes, peeled, deseeded and chopped

salt and freshly ground black pepper

This rich and delicious pie consists of layers of fried aubergine (eggplant), tomato sauce, slices of fontina cheese and a mixture of beaten egg, milk, flour and grated parmesan cheese.

—

Trim the ends off the aubergines, then cut lengthwise into slices 5mm (¼in) thick and sprinkle with salt. Place in a colander set over a bowl and leave for 1 hour to drain off any bitter juices. Rinse off the salt and pat dry, then fry in hot oil until golden on both sides. Drain on paper towels.

To make the tomato sauce, heat the olive oil in a large frying pan over a moderate heat and cook the garlic and oregano for 2 minutes. Add the tomatoes and continue to cook for 15 minutes or until the sauce has thickened. Season with salt and pepper.

Beat the eggs, flour and half of the parmesan together in a bowl, then gradually stir in the milk.

Arrange a layer of fried aubergine slices in the bottom of a well-oiled shallow baking dish. Cover with a layer of tomato sauce and top with slices of fontina cheese. Spoon a little of the egg mixture over the top. Repeat the layers, ending with the egg mixture. Sprinkle the remaining grated parmesan over the top, then bake in a preheated 180°C/350°F/gas 4 oven for 30 minutes or until the top is golden and the sauce is bubbling.

Serves 4–5

Stuffed aubergines

Melitzannes papoutsakia

4 medium aubergines (eggplants), trimmed and cut in half lengthwise

6 tablespoons extra virgin olive oil

1 medium onion, finely chopped

handful of finely chopped flat-leaf parsley

1 teaspoon dried oregano

2 medium tomatoes, peeled, deseeded and grated

4 tablespoons dried breadcrumbs

50g ($\frac{1}{2}$ cup) freshly grated parmesan or kefalotyri cheese

salt and freshly ground black pepper

For the béchamel sauce

2 tablespoons butter

2 tablespoons flour

225g (scant 1 cup) hot milk

1 egg yolk

Melitzanes papoutsakia (literally 'aubergine slippers') are enjoyed by Greeks and Jews alike. The Greek version usually includes a little minced meat, whereas the Jewish version is strictly vegetarian, since the mixing of meat and milk in the same dish is strictly forbidden by Jewish dietary laws.

—

Place the aubergine halves in a large saucepan of lightly salted boiling water, cover and simmer for 5 minutes. Remove and set aside to cool slightly. Gently scoop out the flesh, leaving a shell about 3mm ($\frac{1}{8}$in) thick. Chop the flesh coarsely. Arrange the shells side by side in a well-oiled baking dish.

Heat the olive oil in a large frying pan and cook the onion over a moderate heat until softened. Add the parsley and oregano and cook for another 2 minutes. Add the chopped aubergine flesh and mix well. Cover and cook over a gentle heat for 10 minutes or until tender and starting to turn golden, stirring from time to time. Add the tomatoes and continue to cook, uncovered, for 5 minutes. Remove from the heat and stir in the breadcrumbs and half of the grated cheese. Season with salt and pepper, then fill the aubergine shells with the mixture.

To make the béchamel sauce, melt the butter in a heavy saucepan and stir in the flour. Cook for 1 minute without browning, stirring constantly. Pour in a little hot milk and stir vigorously with a wooden spoon over a moderate heat until the mixture is lump-free. Add the rest of the hot milk, a little at a time, until all incorporated and the sauce is smooth and creamy. Remove from the heat and set aside to cool slightly. Add the egg yolk and season with salt and pepper. Mix well. Spoon a little béchamel over each of the stuffed aubergines and sprinkle the remaining grated cheese on top. Bake in a preheated 180°C/350°F/gas 4 oven for 30 minutes or until bubbling and golden.

Serves 4

Cabbage and walnut strudel

Kaposztas retes

5 tablespoons butter

1 medium onion, chopped

1 small green cabbage, about 1kg ($2\frac{1}{4}$lb), shredded

3 tablespoons raisins

40g ($\frac{1}{3}$ cup) finely chopped walnuts

salt and freshly ground black pepper

3 large sheets fresh or thawed frozen filo pastry

1 tablespoons caraway seeds

Cabbage strudel – or *kroit strudel*, as it is called in Yiddish – makes a delicious snack or light lunch. Using fresh or thawed frozen filo pastry makes it quick and easy to prepare.

—

Melt 3 tablespoons of the butter in a heavy saucepan and add the onion. Cook over a moderate heat until it is translucent. Stir in the cabbage. Cover and cook over a gentle heat for 20–25 minutes or until the cabbage is tender and starting to turn golden, stirring from time to time. Add the raisins and walnuts and season with salt and pepper. Set aside to cool.

Meanwhile, melt the remaining butter and set aside to cool slightly.

Lay a sheet of filo pastry over a clean cloth and brush lightly with melted butter. Place another sheet of pastry on top and brush lightly with melted butter, then repeat with the remaining sheet. Arrange the cabbage mixture over the third of the pastry closest to you. Fold over the edges to seal in the filling. Carefully pick up the corners of the cloth and roll the strudel over once. Brush the top with butter. Lift the cloth again and let the strudel roll over completely. Brush the top with butter. Pick up the cloth-wrapped strudel, then carefully ease the strudel out of the cloth and onto a well-greased baking sheet. Brush the top with butter and sprinkle with caraway seeds. Bake in a preheated 180°C/350°F/gas 4 oven for 20–25 minutes or until the top is golden. Serve hot or warm.

Serves 4

Courgette, tomato and feta gratin

Kalavasutcho

900g (2lb) courgettes (zucchini), trimmed

2–3 tomatoes

225g (8oz) feta cheese, crumbled

2 eggs, lightly beaten

grating of nutmeg

salt and freshly ground black pepper

2 tablespoons freshly grated parmesan or kefalotyri cheese

This recipe comes from Corfu, but variations are made by Jews all over Greece and Turkey.

—

Slice the courgettes thinly lengthwise. Steam for 4–5 minutes, then arrange in a shallow baking dish. Place the tomatoes in a heatproof bowl and cover with boiling water. Set aside for 1–2 minutes until the skins have split. Drain and, when cool enough to handle, peel and slice thinly. Arrange over the courgettes.

In a bowl, mash the feta, then add the eggs. Mix and season with nutmeg, salt and pepper. Pour over the tomatoes and sprinkle the grated cheese on top. Bake in a preheated 180°C/350°F/gas 4 oven for 30 minutes or until golden. Serve hot.

Serves 3–4

Potato and apple latkes

Kartoffel latkes

675g (1½lb) potatoes, coarsely grated

1 small apple, coarsely grated

1 medium onion, finely chopped

2 large eggs, lightly beaten

salt and freshly ground black pepper

olive oil, for shallow-frying

No Jewish cookbook would be complete without kartoffel latkes, the potato pancakes traditionally made for Chanukah.

—

Mix the potatoes, apple, onion and eggs together well. Season with salt and pepper. Heat a thin layer of oil in a heavy frying pan. Working in batches, drop in heaped tablespoonfuls of the mixture and flatten with a fork. Cook over a gentle heat until golden on both sides, then drain on paper towels. Serve hot.

Serves 4

Courgette and potato moussaka

Musaka de kalavasikas

450g (1lb) courgettes (zucchini)

4 tablespoons extra virgin olive oil

450g (1lb) potatoes

1 medium onion, finely chopped

1 teaspoon dried oregano

450g (1lb) ripe plum tomatoes, peeled, deseeded and chopped

pinch of ground cinnamon

75g ($\frac{3}{4}$ cup) freshly grated parmesan or kefalotyri cheese

salt and freshly ground black pepper

For the béchamel sauce

4 tablespoons butter

3 tablespoons flour

450ml (2 cups) hot milk

grating of nutmeg

2 egg yolks

This classic dish from Thessaloniki is perfect for a family dinner or special occasion.

—

Trim the ends off the courgettes, then cut lengthwise into 3mm ($\frac{1}{8}$in) slices. Heat half of the oil in a large frying pan and fry the courgettes in batches until golden on both sides. Drain on paper towels. Meanwhile, cook the potatoes in lightly salted boiling water for 20 minutes or until tender. Drain and, when cool enough to handle, peel and slice fairly thinly.

Heat the remaining olive oil in a large frying pan and add the onion and oregano. Cook over a moderate heat for 5 minutes or until the onion has softened. Add the tomatoes and cinnamon and continue to cook for about 10 minutes or until the sauce starts to thicken. Set aside.

To make the béchamel sauce, melt the butter in a heavy saucepan and stir in the flour. Cook for 1 minute without browning, stirring constantly Pour in a little hot milk and stir vigorously with a wooden spoon over a moderate heat until the mixture is lump-free. Add the rest of the hot milk, a little at a time, until all incorporated and the sauce is smooth and creamy. Add the nutmeg and season with salt and pepper. Allow to cool slightly before stirring in the egg yolks.

Arrange a third of the potatoes over the bottom of a well-oiled baking dish. Cover with a third of the fried courgettes. Spoon over a third of the tomato sauce and one quarter of the grated cheese. Repeat, finishing with tomato sauce and grated cheese. Pour the béchamel over the top and sprinkle over the remaining grated cheese. Bake in a preheated 180°C/350°F/gas 4 oven for 35–40 minutes until the top is golden and the sauce is bubbling.

Serves 4–6

Stuffed courgettes with tomato and pomegranate sauce

Kusa mahshi

8 courgettes (zucchini), about
15–20cm (6–8in) in length

For the filling

200g (1 cup) long-grain rice

2 medium onions, finely chopped

125g (scant 1 cup) cooked and
drained chickpeas (garbanzo
beans)

1 medium tomato, peeled,
deseeded and chopped

2 tablespoons finely chopped
flat-leaf parsley

2 tablespoons finely chopped mint

$\frac{1}{4}$ teaspoon ground cinnamon

$\frac{1}{4}$ teaspoon ground allspice

2 tablespoons extra virgin olive oil

1 tablespoon lemon juice

salt and freshly ground black
pepper

For the sauce

3 tablespoons extra virgin olive oil

1 medium onion, finely chopped

2 garlic cloves, finely chopped

675g ($1\frac{1}{2}$lb) ripe plum tomatoes,
peeled, deseeded and chopped

1 tablespoon pomegranate
molasses

1 teaspoon sugar, or to taste

In this recipe, courgettes (zucchini) are stuffed with rice, chickpeas (garbanzo beans), tomato and herbs and cooked in a delicious tomato sauce flavoured with pomegranate molasses. Pomegranate molasses is widely used in the Middle East to give a tart but fruity flavour to salad dressings, stews, sauces and stuffings. Sometimes it is diluted with a little water, depending on its thickness and strength.

—

Cut off the stem ends of the courgettes. Using an apple corer, carefully scoop out the courgette pulp, leaving a shell 2–3mm ($\frac{1}{8}$in) thick; the pulp is not used for the filling, so save it for a soup or stew.

To make the filling, place the rice, onions, chickpeas, tomato, herbs and spices in a bowl and mix well. Stir in the olive oil and lemon juice and season with salt and pepper. Stuff the courgettes about three-quarters full with the mixture, leaving enough space for the rice to swell during cooking.

To make the sauce, heat the olive oil in a large saucepan or flameproof casserole and add the onion. Cook over a moderate heat until softened. Add the garlic and cook for 2 more minutes. Add the tomatoes and simmer for 10 minutes. Stir in the pomegranate molasses and sugar and simmer for a few more minutes to blend the flavours.

Arrange the stuffed courgettes side by side in one or two layers in the pan with the sauce and add just enough water to cover the courgettes. Bring to the boil, then cover and simmer for 50–60 minutes or until the courgettes are tender and the sauce has reduced. Serve hot.

Serves 4

Leek tapada

Tapada de prasa

900g (2lb) leeks

2 tablespoons extra virgin olive oil

125g (4oz) feta cheese, crumbled

75g ($\frac{3}{4}$ cup) freshly grated parmesan or kachkaval cheese

1 egg, lightly beaten

freshly ground black pepper

For the olive oil pastry

75ml ($\frac{1}{3}$ cup) extra virgin olive oil

75ml ($\frac{1}{3}$ cup) warm water

$\frac{1}{2}$ teaspoon salt

about 250g (2 cups) plain (all-purpose) flour

1 egg, beaten

A *tapada* is a large savoury pie that is traditionally served for the Sabbath and is usually filled with cheese or pureed vegetables. Most of the fillings for *bulemas*, *filas* and *pastels* can also be used for *tapadas*.

—

Trim the ends off the leeks, then cut them in half lengthwise. Wash carefully to remove any grit from between the leaves. Cut into 2cm ($\frac{3}{4}$in) lengths. Heat the olive oil in a large saucepan and add the leeks. Cover and cook over a moderate heat for 10–15 minutes or until tender and starting to turn golden. Place in a bowl and add the feta, parmesan and egg. Mix well and season the filling with pepper.

To make the pastry, mix the oil, water and salt together in a mixing bowl. Gradually add just enough flour to make a soft, malleable dough – start working the flour in with a fork, then use your hands. Divide the dough into two pieces, one slightly larger than the other. Roll out the larger piece into a circle about 30cm (12in) in diameter and 2mm (about $\frac{1}{16}$in) thick. Carefully roll the dough around the rolling pin and unroll it on to a well-oiled 25cm (10in) tart tin. Ease the pastry into the corners, then trim away any excess dough. Prick the bottom with a fork and spoon in the filling.

For the top crust, roll the remaining piece of dough into a circle about 28cm (11in) in diameter. Carefully place on top of the pie and crimp the edges with your fingertips or a fork to seal. Brush with the beaten egg, then bake in a preheated 190°C/375°F/gas 5 oven for 40 minutes or until the crust is golden. Serve hot or warm.

Serves 4–6

Green pie from Thessaloniki
Pastel verde

450g (1lb) mixed greens

about 5 tablespoons extra virgin olive oil

2 spring onions (scallions), thinly sliced

1 leek (including the green part), trimmed and thinly sliced

handful of finely chopped flat-leaf parsley

handful of finely chopped dill

200g (7oz) feta cheese, crumbled

2 eggs

50g ($\frac{1}{2}$ cup) freshly grated parmesan or kefalotyri cheese

salt and freshly ground black pepper

8 or 9 large sheets of fresh or thawed frozen filo pastry

2–3 tablespoons sesame seeds

Pastels (pies) or *pastelikos* (little pies) were traditionally made by the Jews of Thessaloniki for the Sabbath, bar mitzvahs and other special occasions. Most pastels use a simple pastry made from olive oil, flour and water – except for this one, which is always prepared with filo pastry. *Pastel verde* is usually filled with a mixture of spinach, lettuce, leeks, spring onions (scallions) and herbs, but other greens can also be used, such as Swiss chard, beet greens, rocket (arugula), watercress or young, tender dandelion greens.

—

Wash the greens well, then cut into 1cm ($\frac{1}{2}$in) slices. Cook in a covered saucepan for 7–8 minutes or until tender – the water on the leaves is sufficient to prevent scorching. Drain well.

Heat 2 tablespoons of the olive oil in a heavy saucepan and add the spring onions and leek. Cook over a moderate heat until they are starting to turn golden. Add the parsley and dill and cook for a further 3 minutes. Stir in the greens and simmer for 2–3 minutes.

Place the feta, eggs and parmesan in a bowl and mix well. Stir in the greens mixture and season the filling with salt and pepper.

Brush a 23cm (9in) springform cake tin with olive oil. Place a sheet of filo pastry over the top and brush lightly with olive oil. Repeat until half of the filo pastry sheets have been used. Spoon in the filling. Cover with another sheet of filo pastry and brush lightly with olive oil. Repeat until all the sheets of filo pastry have been used. Tuck in the edges of the filo pastry. Sprinkle sesame seeds over the top, then bake in a preheated 180°C/350°F/gas 4 oven for 40–45 minutes or until the top is golden. Remove from the oven, unclip the tin and serve hot.

Serves 4

Swiss chard and white cheese gratin

Antchusa de pazi

675g (1½lb) Swiss chard

125g (4oz) feta or beyaz peynir (Turkish white cheese), mashed with a fork

2 eggs, lightly beaten

75g (¾ cup) freshly grated parmesan or kashkaval cheese

freshly ground black pepper

2 or 3 tablespoons dried breadcrumbs

1–2 tablespoons butter

This classic dairy dish is made with a mixture of Swiss chard, white cheese, beaten eggs and grated cheese. Similar gratins can be made with spinach, pumpkin, leeks, courgettes (zucchini) or aubergine (eggplant).

—

Wash the Swiss chard and remove the stems (you can save them for a soup or stew, if you like). Place the chard leaves in a covered saucepan and cook over a moderate heat for 7–8 minutes or until tender – the water clinging to the leaves is sufficient to prevent scorching. Drain well and chop coarsely.

In a bowl, combine the feta, eggs and 50g (½ cup) of the grated cheese. Season with pepper, then add the chard and mix well. Pour into a well-oiled shallow baking dish. Mix the remaining grated cheese with the breadcrumbs and sprinkle over the top. Dot with butter and bake in a preheated 180°C/350°F/gas 4 oven for 30 minutes or until the top is golden and a knife inserted in the centre comes out clean. Serve hot.

Serves 4

Small white onion tart

Tarte aux oignons nouveaux

3 tablespoons butter

900g (2lb) small white onions, peeled

3 egg yolks

175ml ($\frac{3}{4}$ cup) double (heavy) cream

pinch of ground cinnamon

salt and freshly ground black pepper

For the shortcrust pastry

125g (1 cup) plain (all-purpose) flour

60g ($\frac{1}{2}$ cup) wholemeal (whole wheat) flour

$\frac{1}{4}$ teaspoon salt

100g ($\frac{1}{2}$ cup) butter

1 egg, lightly beaten

1–2 tablespoons iced water

This creamy onion tart from Alsace is often served for the Sabbath.

—

To make the pastry, sift both the flours and salt into a mixing bowl. With your fingertips, rub in the butter until the mixture resembles coarse breadcrumbs. Add the egg and just enough iced water to make a soft ball. Wrap in foil and refrigerate for 1 hour.

Meanwhile, melt the butter in a heavy frying pan and add the onions. Cook over a gentle heat for 30–40 minutes or until very tender and starting to turn golden, stirring from time to time so they cook evenly. Set aside to cool.

Place the chilled pastry dough on a lightly floured surface and knead briefly. Roll out into a circle about 30cm (12in) in diameter. Carefully roll the dough around the rolling pin and unroll onto a greased 23cm (9in) tart tin. Ease the pastry into the corners, then trim away any excess dough. Use a fork to crimp the edges of the pastry and prick the base all over. Cover with a sheet of foil and fill with dried beans – this prevents the tart case from puffing up in the oven. Bake in a preheated 200°C/400°F/gas 6 oven for 8–10 minutes, then remove from the oven and carefully lift out the foil and beans. Turn the oven down to 190°C/375°F/gas 5.

In a large bowl, beat the egg yolks and cream together, then stir in the onions and season with cinnamon, salt and pepper. Pour the filling into the tart case and bake for 30 minutes or until lightly browned and puffed. Serve hot.

Serves 4–6

Mushroom strudel

Gombas retes

3–4 large sheets fresh or thawed frozen filo pastry

2 tablespoons melted butter

2 tablespoons poppy seeds

sour cream or smetana, to serve

For the filling

3 tablespoons butter or olive oil

2–3 shallots, finely chopped

450g (1lb) mushrooms, thinly sliced

handful of finely chopped flat-leaf parsley

1 tablespoon dry white wine, sherry or port

2 teaspoons flour

2 tablespoons sour cream or smetana

1 tablespoon fresh chives, finely chopped

salt and freshly ground black pepper

Mushroom strudel makes a very good snack, as well as a light lunch or supper dish. You can use cultivated or wild mushrooms – whatever is at hand. It is especially good with a dollop of sour cream or smetana on the side.

—

To make the filling, heat the butter in a heavy frying pan and add the shallots. Cook over a moderate until they are softened. Add the mushrooms and parsley and cook for a further 5 minutes or until they are tender. Pour in the wine, then raise the heat and continue to cook until the the liquid has evaporated. Stir in the flour and simmer for 1–2 minutes without browning. Remove from the heat. Add the sour cream and chives and season with salt and pepper. Mix well.

Lay a sheet of filo pastry over a clean cloth and brush lightly with melted butter. Place another sheet of pastry on top and brush with butter, then repeat with the remaining sheet. Spoon the mushroom mixture over the third of the pastry closest to you. Fold over the edges to seal in the filling. Carefully pick up the corners of the cloth and roll the strudel over once. Brush the top with butter. Lift the cloth again and let the strudel roll over completely. Brush the top with butter. Pick up the cloth-wrapped strudel, then carefully ease the strudel out of the cloth and onto a well-greased baking sheet. Brush lightly with butter and sprinkle with poppy seeds.

Bake in a preheated 180°C/350°F/gas 4 oven for 25–30 minutes or until the top is golden. Serve hot with sour cream or smetana on the side.

Serves 3–4

Peppers stuffed with cheese

Pipiruchkas reyenadas de keso

4 red or yellow horn-shaped peppers

225g (8oz) buffalo mozzarella or telemea (Romanian sheep's cheese), sliced fairly thickly

2 tablespoons extra virgin olive oil

2 garlic cloves, finely chopped

1 small onion, finely chopped

350g (12oz) ripe tomatoes, peeled, deseeded and chopped

salt and freshly ground black pepper

In this recipe, the peppers are roasted in the oven, then stuffed with a slice of a sheep's cheese called *telemea* and baked on a bed of tomato sauce. If *telemea* is unavailable, buffalo mozzarella or even feta can be used instead. Long horn-shaped peppers with thin skins – sometimes called Romano peppers – are best for this recipe.

—

Roast the peppers under a hot grill (broiler) until blackened all over, then rinse under cold water and remove the skins. With a sharp knife, cut a slit down the side of each pepper and very carefully remove the core and seeds. Stuff the peppers with the cheese, then brush the tops of the peppers lightly with olive oil.

Heat the remaining olive oil in a heavy frying pan and add the garlic and onion. Cook over a moderate heat until the onion has softened. Add the tomatoes and continue to cook for a further 7–8 minutes or until the sauce has thickened. Season with salt and pepper.

Pour the tomato sauce into the bottom of a shallow baking dish and arrange the stuffed peppers in a single layer on top. Bake in a preheated 180°C/350°F/gas 4 oven for 30 minutes or until the peppers are tender and the cheese has melted. Serve at once.

Serves 4

Potato and mushroom babka

Kartofl babka mit shveml

900g (2lb) potatoes

2–3 tablespoons hot milk

4 tablespoons butter

450g (1lb) mushrooms, thinly sliced

3 tablespoons finely chopped flat-leaf parsley

4 eggs, separated

salt and freshly ground black pepper

sour cream or smetana, to serve

This classic dish is often served with sour cream or smetana on the side.

—

Cook the potatoes in plenty of lightly salted boiling water for 25 minutes or until tender. Drain and, when cool enough to handle, peel and then mash with a potato ricer. Add the milk and half of the butter and mix well.

Melt the remaining butter in a heavy frying pan and add the mushrooms. Cook over a moderate heat until tender, then add to the potato mixture, together with the parsley and egg yolks. Season with salt and pepper. Mix well.

Whisk the egg whites to stiff peaks and fold into the mixture, then pour into a well-buttered baking dish and bake in a preheated 180°C/350°F/gas 4 oven for 40 minutes or until nicely puffed and golden brown on top. Serve at once, with sour cream on the side.

Serves 4–6

Pumpkin triangles

Filas de balkabak

8 large sheets fresh or thawed frozen filo pastry

extra virgin olive oil, for brushing

For the filling

500g (3 cups) cooked pumpkin, blended to a puree

100g (3½ oz) feta or beyaz peynir (Turkish white cheese), mashed with a fork

50g (½ cup) freshly grated parmesan or kashkaval cheese

1 egg, beaten

Filas are paper-thin pastries that the Sephardim adopted from the Turks and made their own, filling them with cheese, spinach, aubergine (eggplant) or pumpkin. Filas are usually small and triangular, but can also be made as one large pie.

—

To make the filling, place the pumpkin puree, feta, parmesan and egg in a bowl and mix well.

Cut the filo pastry into strips about 30cm x 10cm (12in x 4in). Place them in a pile and cover with a cloth to prevent them drying out. Take one strip of filo and brush lightly with olive oil. Place a tablespoon of the filling at the bottom end of the pastry strip. Carefully lift up the right-hand corner and fold over to make a triangle. Brush lightly with olive oil, then fold over again and again until you have reached the top of the pastry strip. Repeat with the remaining filo pastry and filling.

Place the filled pastry triangles on greased baking sheets and brush the tops lightly with olive oil. Bake in a preheated 180°C/350°F/gas 4 oven for 20–25 minutes or until crisp and golden.

Makes about 32 pastries

Potato and carrot kugel

Kartoffel kugel mit mehren

900g (2lb) potatoes, peeled and grated

2 large carrots, grated

2 medium onions, grated

3 eggs, beaten

salt and freshly ground black pepper

4 tablespoons melted butter

All kinds of *kugels* (sweet or savoury puddings) are made in Ashkenazi households, especially with potatoes, apples or *lokshen* (vermicelli). Potato kugel can be made with grated or mashed potatoes. Some cooks add a little grated carrot or apple, others like to thicken the kugel with a little flour or matzo meal. Potato kugel can either be baked in the oven or slowly cooked in a large heavy frying pan on top of the stove until it is crisp and golden on both sides. Traditionally, *kugels* are served for the Sabbath and for Sukkot.

—

Place the potatoes, carrots, onions and eggs in a large bowl and mix well. Season with salt and pepper.

Pour half of the butter into a large shallow baking dish and swirl it around so the base and sides of the dish are well coated. Tip in the potato mixture and drizzle over the remaining butter.

Bake the kugel in a preheated 180°C/350°F/gas 4 oven for 50–60 minutes or until the top is nicely browned. Serve hot.

Serves 4

Potato and spinach croquettes

Fritikas de spinaka kon patatas

225g (8oz) spinach

900g (2lb) potatoes

2 eggs, separated

salt and freshly ground black pepper

flour or matzo meal, for dredging

olive oil, for deep-frying

These delicious little croquettes may be served as a light main course or a side dish. Traditionally they are often prepared for Rosh Hashanah, or for Passover – in which case, matzo meal is used instead of flour.

—

Wash the spinach thoroughly, then cook in a covered saucepan over a moderate heat for 5 minutes or until wilted – the water clinging to the leaves is sufficient to prevent scorching. Drain well and squeeze dry, then chop finely.

Boil the potatoes in plenty of lightly salted water for 25 minutes or until tender. Drain and, when cool enough to handle, peel and then force through a sieve or mash with a potato ricer. Add the spinach and egg yolks and mix well. Season with salt and pepper. Shape into balls the size of a walnut and flatten slightly, then set aside to cool.

Meanwhile, whisk the egg whites until frothy. Dip the croquettes into the egg white then roll in flour. Working in batches, deep-fry the croquettes in hot oil until golden on both sides. Drain on paper towels and serve hot.

Serves 4–5

Vegetable gratin for Shavuot

Gratin de Chavuot

450g (1lb) courgettes (zucchini)

450g (1lb) aubergines (eggplants)

about 150ml ($\frac{2}{3}$ cup) extra virgin olive oil

2 large onions, thinly sliced

450g (1lb) ripe tomatoes, peeled, deseeded and chopped

150g (1$\frac{1}{2}$ cups) grated gruyère or parmesan cheese

2 tablespoons torn basil leaves

salt and freshly ground black pepper

3 tablespoons dried breadcrumbs

This delicious gratin from Provence consists of layers of courgettes (zucchini), aubergines (eggplants), onions, sliced tomatoes and grated cheese. If you like, you can fry the courgette and aubergine slices, but I prefer to grill (broil) them, as this uses less oil.

—

Trim the ends off the courgettes and peel the aubergines, then cut both lengthwise into slices about 5mm ($\frac{1}{4}$in) thick. Arrange the slices on a well-oiled sheet of foil and brush liberally with olive oil, then roast under a hot grill (broiler) until golden brown. Turn over and repeat on the other side.

Meanwhile, heat 3 tablespoons olive oil in a large frying pan and add the onions. Cook over a moderate heat until they start to turn golden, stirring from time to time so they cook evenly. Add the tomatoes and continue to cook for 7–8 minutes or until the sauce is thickened.

In a well-oiled shallow baking dish, arrange the courgettes, aubergines and onion and tomato sauce in layers, sprinkling each layer with grated cheese and torn basil leaves and seasoning with salt and pepper. Mix the breadcrumbs with the remaining cheese and sprinkle over the top. Drizzle over 2 tablespoons olive oil, then bake in a preheated 180°C/350°F/gas 4 oven for 45 minutes or until golden. Serve hot.

Serves 4

Eggs

'Love and eggs are best when they are fresh'

YIDDISH PROVERB

As a symbol of fertility and eternity since Biblical times, eggs have always been significant in Jewish culture and tradition. In the past, eggs – especially raw eggs with double yolks – were often given to young brides to increase their fertility and protect them from evil. Eggs are also traditionally prepared after funerals, since they are a symbol of death and mourning, as well as the continuance of life.

The egg is one of the most versatile foods. Not only is it a complete food in itself, but it can be boiled, baked, fried, poached, scrambled or made into omelettes. Sephardic Jews have a unique way of preparing eggs for the Sabbath called *huevos haminados*, or hamine eggs. Whole eggs are simmered very slowly overnight with a little oil and some onion skins until their shells turn dark brown – sometimes coffee grounds are added to enhance the colour. Originally, they were baked in an oven, covered with embers, which explains the literal translation of their name: 'oven eggs'.

Scrambled eggs with hot sauce

Ojja

3 tablespoons extra virgin olive oil

6 garlic cloves, finely chopped

1 tablespoon concentrated tomato puree (paste), dissolved in a little hot water

1–2 teaspoons harissa (see page 36), to taste

½ teaspoon ground caraway seeds

½ teaspoon ground coriander seeds

½ teaspoon paprika

salt

8 eggs, beaten

2 tablespoons finely chopped flat-leaf parsley

In this recipe, eggs are scrambled with a spicy hot sauce made with tomato puree, harissa, plenty of garlic, ground caraway and coriander, which gives them a delicious flavour and a vibrant orange colour.

—

Heat the olive oil in a heavy saucepan, add the garlic and cook over a moderate heat for 1–2 minutes without browning. Add the diluted tomato puree, harissa and spices, then season with salt and mix well. Bring to the boil and simmer for 5 minutes.

Add the eggs and cook over a gentle heat, stirring constantly with a wooden spoon, until the eggs have a creamy consistency. Serve at once, garnished with parsley.

Serves 4–6

Scrambled eggs with onions

Oeufs brouillés a l'oignon

3 tablespoons extra virgin olive oil

2 large onions, chopped

2 tablespoons finely chopped flat-leaf parsley

$\frac{1}{2}$ teaspoon ground turmeric

salt and freshly ground black pepper

6 eggs, beaten

This dish makes a lovely light lunch or snack. A similar dish (*eier mit zwiebel*) is prepared by Ashkenazi Jews – but without the turmeric.

—

Heat the olive oil in a heavy frying pan and add the onions. Cook over a gentle heat until they have softened, stirring from time to time so they cook evenly. Add the parsley and turmeric, then season with salt and pepper and cook for 3 minutes. Pour in the eggs and cook over a gentle heat, stirring with a wooden spoon, until the eggs have a creamy consistency. Serve at once.

Serves 4

Little cheese omelettes

Ejjeh ab jiben

3 large eggs

1–2 garlic cloves, crushed

225g (8oz) feta cheese, crumbled

$\frac{1}{4}$ teaspoon ground allspice

freshly ground black pepper

extra virgin olive oil, for frying

These delicious little fritters or omelettes are traditionally served for Shavuot. They also make a delicious lunch with lightly toasted pita bread, a green salad and olives on the side.

—

Beat the eggs in a bowl and add the garlic, feta and allspice. Mix well and season with pepper. Cook the omelettes in batches: heat a thin layer of olive oil in a heavy frying pan, then add tablespoonfuls of the mixture and flatten with the back of a spoon. Cook over a moderate heat until golden on both sides. Repeat until all the omelettes are cooked, adding more oil to the pan as necessary. Serve hot.

Serves 4

Baked eggs in spicy tomato sauce

Huevos kon tomates

2 tablespoons extra virgin olive oil

3 spring onions (scallions), finely chopped

450g (1lb) tomatoes, peeled, deseeded and chopped

½ teaspoon ground turmeric

½ teaspoon ground cumin

4 eggs

2 tablespoons finely chopped flat-leaf parsley

salt and freshly ground black pepper

This everyday dish from Izmir is usually served with a bowl of chilled yoghurt on the side. Sometimes the spices are omitted and a thin slice of cheese, such as kashkaval or emmenthal, is placed over the eggs during cooking.

—

Heat the olive oil in a large frying pan and add the spring onions. Cook over a moderate heat until they start to turn golden. Add the tomatoes and spices and continue to cook for 10 minutes or until the sauce starts to thicken.

With the back of a spoon, make four indentations in the sauce. Carefully break an egg into each depression. Sprinkle over the parsley and season with salt and pepper. Cover with a tight-fitting lid and cook over a gentle heat until the eggs have set, about 4–5 minutes. Serve at once.

Serves 2–4

Iranian potato cake

Kuku-ye sibzamini

450g (1lb) 'floury' potatoes

1 medium onion, grated

4 eggs, beaten

50g (2 cups) finely chopped
flat-leaf parsley

$\frac{1}{2}$ teaspoon ground turmeric

$\frac{1}{4}$ teaspoon ground cardamom

salt and freshly ground black
pepper

2–3 tablespoons ghee, butter or
olive oil

Iranian Jews have a wide repertoire of *kuku* (omelettes),
which they often prepare for the Sabbath. This one, made with
potatoes, onion, parsley and spices, is very light and delicious.

—

Peel the potatoes and grate them coarsely. Place in a bowl,
together with the onion, eggs, parsley, turmeric and cardamom.
Mix well and season with salt and pepper.

Heat the ghee in a large, heavy frying pan and pour in the egg
mixture. Cover and cook over a gentle heat until the bottom is
golden. Carefully slide the kuku onto a saucepan lid or plate.
Place the frying pan over the uncooked side of the kuku and hold
the pan firmly against the saucepan lid. Quickly flip both the
frying pan and the lid over, so that the uncooked side of the kuku
sits on the bottom of the frying pan. Continue cooking the kuku
until the bottom is golden. Slide onto a serving platter and serve
hot, cut into wedges like a pie.

Serves 4

Little courgette and spring onion omelettes

Ejjeh kusa

2–3 small courgettes (zucchini), about 350g (12oz)

4 eggs

3 spring onions (scallions), thinly sliced

3 tablespoons finely chopped fresh mint leaves

handful of finely chopped flat-leaf parsley

2 garlic cloves, finely chopped

2 tablespoons flour

$\frac{1}{4}$ teaspoon ground cinnamon

$\frac{1}{4}$ teaspoon ground allspice

salt and freshly ground black pepper

olive oil, for frying

These little omelettes make a very good snack, light lunch or supper dish. They are also often made for the Sabbath, bar mitzvahs or other special occasions, because they can be served hot or cold. Alternatively, you can prepare this recipe as one large omelette – like a Persian *kuku* – and serve it cut into bite-sized pieces.

—

Trim the ends off the courgettes, then grate them coarsely. Place in a sieve set over a bowl and press down on the grated courgettes to squeeze out any excess moisture.

Beat the eggs in a large bowl and add the courgettes, spring onions, herbs, garlic, flour and spices and mix well. Season with salt and pepper.

Cook the omelettes in batches: heat a thin layer of olive oil in a heavy frying pan, then add tablespoonfuls of the courgette mixture and flatten with the back of a spoon. Cook over a moderate heat until golden on both sides. Repeat until all the omelettes are cooked, adding more oil to the pan as necessary. Serve hot or cold.

Serves 4

Herb omelette with walnuts and barberries

Kuku sabzi

3 spring onions (scallions), very finely chopped

50g (1 cup) finely chopped flat-leaf parsley, leaves picked and finely chopped

25g ($\frac{1}{2}$ cup) finely chopped dill

25g ($\frac{1}{2}$ cup) finely chopped coriander (cilantro)

2 tablespoons freshly shelled walnuts, finely ground in a blender or food processor

1–2 tablespoons dried barberries or cranberries, to taste

4 eggs

1–2 teaspoons flour

$\frac{1}{2}$ teaspoon ground turmeric

$\frac{1}{2}$ teaspoon ground cinnamon

$\frac{1}{2}$ teaspoon ground coriander

salt and freshly ground black pepper

3 tablespoons butter, ghee or olive oil

This is one of the most well known omelettes in the Iranian Jewish repertoire, and is often prepared for the Sabbath. It is made from a variety of herbs and greens, such as flat-leaf parsley, coriander (cilantro), dill, lettuce and spring onions (scallions), though the exact proportions vary, according to what is at hand. In this recipe, barberries add a deliciously tart flavour. Kuku sabzi is very good served with drinks, in which case it is usually cut into small squares and garnished with chopped walnuts.

—

Place the spring onions and herbs in a bowl and mix well, then stir in the walnuts and barberries.

Beat the eggs in a large bowl with the flour and spices. Add the herb and walnut mixture and mix well. Season with salt and pepper.

Heat the butter in a heavy frying pan and, when it is hot, pour in the egg mixture. Cover and cook over a gentle heat for 15–20 minutes or until the bottom is golden. Place under a hot grill (broiler) for 20 seconds to set the top, then slide the kuku onto a saucepan lid or plate. Place the frying pan over the uncooked side of the kuku and hold the pan firmly against the saucepan lid. Quickly flip both the frying pan and the lid over, so that the uncooked side of the kuku sits on the bottom of the frying pan. Continue cooking the omelette over a gentle heat on the hob until the bottom is golden. Slide onto a serving platter and serve hot, cut into wedges like a pie.

Serves 4

Spinach frittata with raisins and pine nuts

Frittata di spinaci

450g (1lb) spinach

3 tablespoons extra virgin olive oil

1 small onion, finely chopped

3 tablespoons raisins

3 tablespoons pine nuts

3 eggs

2 teaspoons matzo meal

grating of nutmeg

salt and freshly ground black pepper

1 tablespoon butter

1–2 tablespoons sugar, to taste

This frittata from Venice is traditionally prepared during Passover. It is usually served cold and lightly dusted with sugar, but is also very good hot.

—

Wash the spinach thoroughly, then cook in a covered saucepan over a moderate heat for 5–7 minutes or until tender – the water clinging to the leaves is sufficient to prevent scorching. Drain well, squeezing out as much moisture as you can. Chop finely.

Heat 2 tablespoons of the olive oil in a heavy frying pan, add the onion and cook over a moderate heat until softened. Stir in the raisins and pine nuts and continue to cook until the pine nuts turn golden. Stir in the spinach and cook over a gentle heat for 2–3 minutes to blend the flavours.

Beat the eggs in a large bowl, then stir in the spinach mixture and matzo meal. Season with nutmeg, salt and pepper.

In the same frying pan, heat the remaining olive oil and the butter and, when it is hot, pour in the egg mixture. Cook over a gentle heat for 15–20 minutes or until the bottom is golden. Place under a hot grill (broiler) for 20 seconds to set the top, then carefully slide the frittata onto a saucepan lid or plate. Place the frying pan over the uncooked side of the frittata and hold the pan firmly against the saucepan lid. Quickly flip both the frying pan and the lid over, so that the uncooked side of the frittata sits on the bottom of the frying pan. Continue cooking the frittata over a gentle heat on the hob until the bottom is golden. Slide onto a serving platter and sprinkle with sugar. Serve hot or cold, cut into wedges like a pie.

Serves 4

Baked artichoke tortino

Tortino di carciofi

4 artichokes

1 lemon, cut in half

flour or matzo meal, for dusting

olive oil, for deep-frying

4 eggs

2 tablespoons double (heavy) cream

salt and freshly ground black pepper

This dish from Tuscany is often prepared during Passover, when artichokes are in season – in which case, matzo meal is used instead of flour.

—

Trim and peel the stems of the artichokes, then remove all the outer tough, inedible leaves. Cut the artichokes in half and remove the fuzzy chokes. Rub the artichoke bottoms all over with the lemon halves to prevent them from blackening, then cut into 5mm ($\frac{1}{4}$in) slices. Dust with flour and deep-fry in hot oil until golden on both sides. Drain on paper towels.

Beat the eggs and cream together in a bowl and season with salt and pepper.

Arrange the artichoke slices in the bottom of a shallow baking dish and pour over the egg mixture. Bake in a preheated 190°C/375°F/gas 5 oven for 25–30 minutes or until the top is golden and the eggs are set. Serve at once.

Serves 4

Aubergine and white cheese fritada

Fritada de berenjena

2 large aubergines (eggplants), about 675g (1½lb)

2 tablespoons extra virgin olive oil

150g (5oz) feta or beyaz peynir (Turkish white cheese), mashed with a fork

3 eggs

3 tablespoons freshly grated parmesan or kefalotyri cheese

salt and freshly ground black pepper

The Sephardic fritada is related to the Italian frittata, but it is usually baked rather than cooked on top of the stove. Fritadas are generally made with spinach, Swiss chard, potatoes, pumpkin, leeks or courgettes (zucchini). Sometimes a little mashed potato or matzo meal is added, especially during Passover.

—

Roast the whole aubergines under a hot grill (broiler) until they are soft and the skins are blackened all over. When cool enough to handle, scoop out the flesh. Don't worry if a little of the blackened skin is mixed in – it only adds to the flavour. Put the flesh in a bowl and mash with a fork. Add the olive oil and mix well.

Add the feta to the aubergine mixture, together with the eggs and half the grated cheese. Season with salt and pepper. Pour into a well-buttered baking dish and sprinkle the remaining grated cheese on top. Bake in a preheated 180°C/350°F/gas 4 oven for 40–45 minutes or until the top is golden brown. Serve hot.

Serves 4

Leek and potato fritada

Fritada di prassa

450g (1lb) leeks

1 medium potato, about 225g (8oz)

3 large eggs

3 tablespoons olive oil

75g (¾ cup) freshly grated parmesan or kefalotyri cheese

2 tablespoons finely chopped flat-leaf parsley

grating of nutmeg

salt and freshly ground black pepper

Traditionally served as part of a dairy meal, especially during Passover, this simple fritada from Thessaloniki is very light and easy to prepare.

—

Trim the ends off the leeks, then slice thinly, including some of the dark green parts. Steam for 10–15 minutes or until the leeks are very tender. When cool enough to handle, squeeze out as much liquid as you can.

Meanwhile, cook the potato in plenty of lightly salted boiling water until tender. Drain and, when cool enough to handle, peel and then mash with a potato ricer. Add the leeks, eggs, olive oil, 50g (½ cup) of the grated cheese and parsley. Season with nutmeg, salt and pepper and mix well.

Pour into a well-oiled shallow baking dish. Sprinkle over the remaining cheese. Bake in a preheated 180°C/350°F/gas 4 oven for 40–45 minutes or until the top is golden brown. Serve hot.

Serves 4

Provençal green omelette
Omelette verte

225g (8oz) Swiss chard

a handful of flat-leaf parsley, stems removed

2 tablespoons basil leaves

1 teaspoon marjoram leaves

1 garlic clove, crushed

4 large eggs

grating of nutmeg

salt and freshly ground black pepper

2 tablespoons extra virgin olive oil

This delicious omelette from Provence is often prepared for Rosh Hashanah. It can be made with Swiss chard, spinach or beetroot (beet) greens or a mixture of all three.

—

Wash the Swiss chard, then cut away the stalks and any thick ribs (reserve these for a soup or stew). Cook the leaves in a covered saucepan over a moderate heat for 7–8 minutes or until tender – the water clinging to the leaves is sufficient to prevent scorching. Drain well and chop coarsely.

Crush the herbs and garlic in a mortar with a pestle until they form a thick, green puree. Beat the eggs in a bowl, then stir in the herb mixture and chopped Swiss chard. Mix well and season with nutmeg, salt and pepper.

Heat the olive oil in a heavy frying pan and, when it is hot, pour in the egg mixture. Cook over a gentle heat until the bottom is golden. Place under a hot grill (broiler) for 20 seconds to set the top, then carefully slide the omelette onto a saucepan lid or plate. Place the frying pan over the uncooked side of the omelette and hold the pan firmly against the saucepan lid. Quickly flip both the frying pan and the lid over, so that the uncooked side of the omelette sits on the bottom of the frying pan. Continue cooking the omelette over a gentle heat on the hob until the bottom is golden. Slide onto a serving platter and serve hot, cut into wedges like a pie.

Serves 4

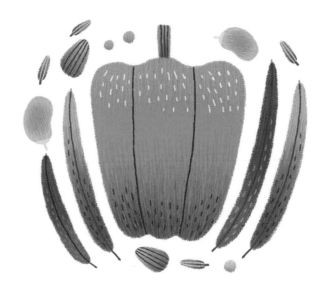

Vegetables

'Hunger is the best seasoning'

JEWISH PROVERB

The Jews are well known for their love of vegetables, especially the artichoke and the aubergine (eggplant) – so much so that in Italy the aubergine was often historically referred to as 'the food of the Jews'. Middle Eastern Jews have been enthusiastic onion and garlic eaters since Biblical times. And Jews everywhere from India to North Africa enjoy stuffed vegetables, fritters, croquettes and especially sweet and sour vegetables. In fact many Italian sweet and sour dishes are named *all'ebraica* or *alla giudea* (Jewish style).

Jewish merchants from Spain were instrumental in introducing vegetables from the New World – tomatoes, corn, beans and potatoes, as well as sweet and hot peppers – to the rest of the Mediterranean. Jews were quick to adopt these and, when the Sephardim fled Spain during the Inquisition, they took these new vegetables too, along with the knowledge of how to prepare them.

Vegetables play an important part in many Jewish holiday celebrations. Simple stews made of vegetables or pulses are traditionally served to break the fast of Tisha Be-Av, when the eating of meat or fish is prohibited. All kinds of stuffed vegetables or vegetable stews are made for Sukkot, the Harvest Festival. Ashkenazi Jews often serve *holishkes* (stuffed cabbage) and Algerian Jews make loubia (white beans simmered in spicy tomato sauce), while Balkan Jews prepare a mixed vegetable stew called giuvech. During Rosh Hashanah, green vegetables such as spinach, green beans, cabbage, courgettes (zucchini) and broad (fava) beans are served to symbolize rebirth and renewal. In Tunisia, broad beans are served at the start of most Jewish festivals: since they are traditionally known as a food of the poor, they serve as a reminder of the dispossessed and less fortunate in the world; it is also said that the bean represents the Jew, and the pod is a symbol of divine protection.

Artichoke and broad bean tajine with green olives and ginger

Tajine d'artichauts et de feves

9 frozen artichoke bottoms, thawed and cut into quarters

200g (1½ cups) freshly shelled or frozen baby broad (fava) beans

6 tablespoons extra virgin olive oil

1 garlic clove, finely chopped

1 teaspoon freshly grated ginger

½ teaspoon ground turmeric

about 225ml (scant 1 cup) vegetable stock or water

75g (⅓ cup) green olives, pitted and cut in half

juice of ½ lemon

salt and freshly ground black pepper

2 tablespoons finely chopped flat-leaf parsley or coriander (cilantro)

The springtime combination of artichokes and broad (fava) beans is much loved all around the Mediterranean. In this recipe from Morocco, the vegetables are simmered with olive oil, ginger, turmeric, green olives and lemon juice, which gives them a lovely depth of flavour.

—

Place the artichoke bottoms, broad beans, olive oil, garlic, ginger and turmeric in a heavy saucepan and add the stock. Bring to the boil, then cover and simmer for 30–40 minutes or until the vegetables are tender and the sauce has reduced. Add the olives and lemon juice and season with salt and pepper. Simmer, uncovered, for a further 10 minutes to blend the flavours. Serve hot, garnished with parsley.

Serves 4

Asparagus gratin

Asparagi al gratin

900g (2lb) asparagus

3 tablespoons dried breadcrumbs

1–2 tablespoons butter

For the béchamel sauce

4 tablespoons butter

3 tablespoons flour

450ml (2 cups) hot milk

grating of nutmeg

salt and freshly ground black pepper

3 tablespoons freshly grated parmesan cheese

Traditionally served as part of a Thursday night dairy meal, this makes a very good light lunch or side dish.

—

Trim the ends off the asparagus and peel any fibrous inedible parts from the lower stalks. Steam for 15–20 minutes or until just tender.

Meanwhile, to make the béchamel sauce, melt the butter in a heavy saucepan and stir in the flour. Cook for 1 minute without browning, stirring constantly. Pour in a little hot milk and stir vigorously with a wooden spoon over a moderate heat until the mixture is free from lumps. Add the rest of the hot milk, a little at a time, until it is all incorporated and the sauce is smooth and creamy. Season with nutmeg, salt and pepper. Remove from the heat and stir in the parmesan cheese.

Pour a little of the sauce into the bottom of a well-buttered shallow baking dish. Arrange the asparagus on top and pour over the remaining béchamel sauce. Sprinkle the breadcrumbs over the top and dot with butter. Bake in a preheated 190°F/375°F/gas 5 oven for 20–25 minutes or until the top is golden. Serve hot.

Serves 4

Sweet aubergine fritters

Papeyado de berendjena

4 medium aubergines
(eggplants), about 900g (2lb)

salt

2 eggs, lightly beaten

olive oil for deep-frying

sugar, for dusting

These lovely fritters are traditionally made for Rosh Hashanah. They are usually served with a dusting of sugar – to symbolize a sweet New Year. Sometimes the fritters are layered with a sprinkling of sugar and baked in the oven until the sugar is caramelized. Similar fritters can also be made with slices of pumpkin.

—

Trim the ends of the aubergines and cut into rounds about 5mm ($\frac{1}{4}$ inch thick). Sprinkle with salt and set in a colander for 1 hour to release the bitter juices. Wash off the salt and pat dry.

Dip the slices into beaten egg and deep-fry in batches in hot oil until they are golden on both sides. Drain on paper towels. Serve hot, dusted with sugar.

Serves 4 to 6

Sweet and sour green beans

Ziss-sauer grune bohnen

450g (1lb) green beans

2 tablespoons butter

1–2 teaspoons sugar, to taste

3 tablespoons cider vinegar

salt and freshly ground black
pepper

Cut of the ends off the green beans and remove any strings along the sides, then cut into 4cm ($1\frac{1}{2}$in) lengths. Steam for 10–15 minutes or until they are tender.

Melt the butter in a large frying pan and stir in the sugar and vinegar. Add the green beans and stir well, so they are evenly coated in the sauce. Season with salt and pepper and simmer for 3–4 minutes to blend the flavours. Serve at once.

Serves 4

Aubergines with onions, tomatoes and red chillies

Mussaka'a batinjan

900g (2lb) small aubergines
(eggplants)

salt

olive oil, for frying

3 medium onions, chopped

3 garlic cloves, finely chopped

2–3 red chillies, deseeded and
finely chopped

450g (1lb) tomatoes, peeled,
deseeded and roughly chopped

This dish is often served for the Sabbath, as it can be made
in advance and served cold the following day. This dish is also
very good served hot with a rice pilaf.

—

Trim the ends off the aubergines, then cut into rounds about
5mm ($\frac{1}{4}$in) thick and sprinkle with salt. Place in a colander set
over a bowl and leave for 1 hour to drain off any bitter juices.
Rinse off the salt and pat dry, then fry in hot oil until golden
on both sides. Drain on paper towels.

Add 2 tablespoons oil to the same pan, then add the onions,
garlic and chillies. Cook over a moderate heat until the onions
start to turn golden, stirring from time to time so they cook
evenly. Add the tomatoes and cook over a gentle heat for 10
minutes. Add the fried aubergines and simmer for 10 more
minutes or until the flavours are blended. Serve hot or cold.

Serves 4–6

Aubergine rolls stuffed with white cheese

Yaprakes de berenjena

2–3 large aubergines (eggplants), about 900g (2lb)

olive oil, for brushing

225g (8oz) feta or beyaz peynir (Turkish white cheese), mashed with a fork

1 egg, plus 1 egg yolk, lightly beaten together

salt and freshly ground black pepper

flat-leaf parsley, to serve

This dish is very good served as a light lunch, perhaps with a little tomato sauce or salad on the side. It consists of slices of roasted aubergine (eggplant), topped with a mixture of a fresh white cheese called beyaz peynir and eggs, then rolled up and baked in the oven.

—

Trim the ends off the aubergines, then cut lengthwise into slices about 5mm ($\frac{1}{4}$in) thick. Spread out the slices on a well-oiled baking tray and brush lightly with oil. Roast under a hot grill (broiler) until the slices are golden on both sides.

Mix the feta and beaten egg in a bowl and season with salt and pepper. Spoon a little of this filling onto one end of each slice of aubergine, then roll up. Arrange the stuffed aubergine rolls in a single layer in a well-oiled shallow baking dish. Bake in a preheated 180°C/350°F/gas 4 oven for 15–20 minutes or until the cheese has melted. Serve hot, sprinkled with parsley.

Serves 4

North African white beans in hot sauce

Loubia

225g (1 cup) dried white haricot or cannellini beans

2 tablespoons extra virgin olive oil

1 medium onion, chopped

4–5 garlic cloves, finely chopped

3 ripe tomatoes, peeled, deseeded and chopped

2 teaspoons harissa (see page 36), or to taste

1 bay leaf

1 teaspoon paprika

$\frac{1}{2}$ teaspoon ground cumin

salt and freshly ground black pepper

3 tablespoons finely chopped flat-leaf parsley or coriander (cilantro)

This dish is much loved by Tunisian and Algerian Jews, who often serve it for the Sabbath. It is made with white beans simmered in an onion and tomato sauce that is strongly spiced with garlic, cumin and harissa.

—

Soak the beans overnight, then drain.

Heat the olive oil in a saucepan and add the onion. Cook over a moderate heat until it starts to soften, then add the garlic and cook for 1–2 more minutes. Add the beans, tomatoes, harissa, bay leaf and spices. Pour in enough hot water to cover the beans by about 2cm ($\frac{3}{4}$in) and bring to the boil. Cover and simmer for 1–1$\frac{1}{2}$ hours or until the beans are tender and the sauce has thickened. Season with salt and pepper.

Serve hot, garnished with parsley.

Serves 4

Sweet and sour red cabbage with apples and juniper berries

Kyslo sladka kapusta s jablka

1 head red cabbage, about 900g (2lb)

2 tart apples

3 tablespoons butter

1 large onion, thinly sliced

$\frac{1}{4}$ teaspoon cloves

3–4 juniper berries

4 tablespoons hot water

1 tablespoon brown sugar

2 tablespoons cider vinegar, or to taste

salt and freshly ground black pepper

Variations of this dish – called *Rote kroit mit apfeln* in Yiddish – are made throughout Central Europe. In this recipe from the Slovak Republic, the cabbage is simmered in butter with onion, apple, cider vinegar and sugar. In Germany, caraway seeds are often added, or a few raisins to enhance the sweetness, while in Alsace it is sometimes made with red wine instead of water.

—

Cut away the hard core from the cabbage, then shred finely. Peel, core and slice the apples fairly thickly.

Heat the butter in a heavy saucepan and add the onion. Cook over a moderate heat until it starts to turn golden. Add the cabbage, apples, cloves, juniper berries and the hot water and bring to the boil. Cover and simmer for 50 minutes or until the cabbage is very soft, adding a little more water if necessary.

Mix the sugar with the cider vinegar and add to the cabbage. Season with salt and pepper, then simmer for 5 more minutes to blend the flavours. Serve hot.

Serves 4–6

Cabbage stuffed with rice, chickpeas and raisins

Malfoof

1 large head green cabbage, about 1.5kg (3lb), cored and leaves loosened without being removed

salt and freshly ground black pepper

For the stuffing

125g ($\frac{2}{3}$ cup) long-grain rice

125g ($\frac{2}{3}$ cup) cooked and drained chickpeas (garbanzo beans)

2 medium onions, finely chopped

4 tablespoons raisins

25g ($\frac{1}{2}$ cup) finely chopped flat-leaf parsley

$\frac{1}{4}$ teaspoon ground allspice

$\frac{1}{4}$ teaspoon ground cinnamon

2 tablespoons extra virgin olive oil

For the tomato and tamarind sauce

2 tablespoons extra virgin olive oil

2 garlic cloves, finely chopped

250g (1$\frac{1}{2}$ cups) canned plum tomatoes, forced through a sieve or pureed in a food processor

225ml (1 cup) hot water

1–2 teaspoons tamarind paste, diluted in a little hot water

In this dish, cabbage leaves are stuffed with a mixture of rice, chickpeas, onions, raisins and spices, and simmered in a tomato sauce flavoured with tamarind, which gives it a delicious sweet and sour flavour. *Malfoof* is often served for Sukkot.

—

Place the cabbage in a large saucepan of lightly salted boiling water and cook for 7–8 minutes or until the outer leaves are pliable. Lift out the cabbage and cool slightly, then remove the outer leaves without tearing them and return the cabbage to the pan. Repeat until all the leaves have been cooked and removed. The larger leaves will be stuffed, but reserve some smaller inner leaves too.

To make the stuffing, cook the rice in lightly salted boiling water for 10–15 minutes. Drain well and mix with the chickpeas, onions, raisins, parsley, spices and olive oil. Season with salt and pepper.

To make the sauce, heat the olive oil in a saucepan and cook the garlic over a moderate heat for 1–2 minutes without browning. Add the tomatoes and water and bring to the boil. Stir in the tamarind and season with salt and pepper. Simmer for 5 minutes. Meanwhile, working with one leaf at a time, and with the stem end of the leaf nearest you, place about 2 heaped tablespoonfuls (depending on the size of the leaf) of the filling close to the stem and fold over the sides to enclose the filling. Roll up the leaf away from you, towards the tip, to form a parcel.

Pour a little sauce into a large pan and cover with the reserved smaller leaves. Arrange the stuffed cabbage leaves side by side, seam side down, over the top, pouring a little sauce over each row. Pour over the remaining sauce and place an inverted, small heatproof plate on top to prevent the parcels from unrolling. Cover the pan and bring to the boil. Simmer for 1 hour or until the parcels are tender. Transfer to a serving platter and serve hot.

Serves 4–6

Carrot tzimmes

Mehren tzimmes

450g (1lb) carrots

2 tablespoons butter

2 teaspoons flour

1 tablespoon sugar

pinch of ground cinnamon

salt and freshly ground black pepper

125ml ($\frac{1}{2}$ cup) hot water

This staple of the Ashkenazi kitchen is usually served for Friday night dinner, and for the New Year – its sweetness, and the resemblance of the carrots to gold coins, symbolize the hope of a prosperous year to come.

—

Trim the ends off the carrots, then cut into 5mm ($\frac{1}{4}$in) rounds.

Melt the butter in a heavy saucepan and add the carrots. Mix well, so they are evenly coated in butter. Stir in the flour and cook for 1 minute without browning. Add the sugar and cinnamon and season to taste. Add the hot water and simmer, stirring constantly, for 5 minutes or until the carrots are tender and the sauce has thickened. Serve hot.

Serves 4

Courgettes with onions, tomatoes and harissa

Courgettes aux oignons et aux tomates

3–4 medium courgettes (zucchini)

3 tablespoons extra virgin olive oil

1 large onion, thinly sliced

3 garlic cloves, finely chopped

4 ripe tomatoes, peeled and chopped

1–2 teaspoons harissa (see page 36), or to taste

5–6 tablespoons hot water

salt

This dish is very good served on its own, or with rice or couscous.

—

Trim the ends off the courgettes, then cut into 1cm ($\frac{1}{2}$in) rounds.

Heat the olive oil in a large frying pan and add the onion. Cook over a moderate heat until it starts to turn golden, then add the garlic and cook for 2 more minutes.

Add the courgettes, tomatoes, harissa and the hot water. Season with salt and bring to the boil. Cover and simmer for 30–40 minutes or until the courgettes are tender and the sauce has reduced. Serve hot.

Serves 4

Cauliflower simmered with onions, tomatoes and cumin

Brouklou bsal wa tomatich

1 medium cauliflower

3 tablespoons extra virgin olive oil

2 medium onions, chopped

4 ripe tomatoes, peeled, deseeded and chopped

1 teaspoon ground cumin

1–2 teaspoons harissa (see page 36), or to taste

salt

In this recipe the cauliflower is first steamed, then simmered in a delicious onion and tomato sauce strongly spiced with harissa.

—

Trim the stalk off the cauliflower, then break into florets. Steam for 5–6 minutes or until just tender.

Heat the olive oil in a large frying pan and add the onions. Cook over a moderate heat until they are softened. Add the tomatoes, cumin, harissa and season with salt. Cook for further 10 minutes, then add the cauliflower florets and simmer for a few more minutes to blend the flavours. Serve hot.

Serves 4–6

Sephardic stewed lentils

Lentejas a la djudia

300g (1½ cups) green lentils

about 600ml (2½ cups) hot water

3 tablespoons extra virgin olive oil

2 medium onions, finely chopped

4 ripe tomatoes, peeled, deseeded and chopped

¼ teaspoon ground cumin

salt

kirmizi biber or dried chilli flakes

handful of finely chopped flat-leaf parsley

Traditionally served to break the fast of Tisha Be-Av, this dish is very good with a rice pilaf. Kirmizi biber is a kind of mild to hot chilli that is widely used in Turkish cooking, either crushed into flakes or ground into a powder. It can be found in most Turkish stores, but if unavailable dried chilli flakes may be used instead.

—

Soak the lentils for 2 hours, then drain. Place in a saucepan, cover with the hot water and bring to the boil. Cover and simmer for 1 hour or until almost tender, adding more hot water if necessary. Drain and reserve 90ml (⅓ cup) of the cooking liquid.

Meanwhile, heat the olive oil in a saucepan and add the onions. Cook over a moderate heat until they start to soften. Add the tomatoes and cumin and continue to cook for 7 minutes or until the sauce starts to thicken. Add the lentils and reserved cooking liquid and bring to the boil. Season with salt and kirmizi biber or chilli flakes, then cover and simmer for another 10 minutes or until the lentils are tender and the sauce has reduced. Just before serving, stir in the parsley. Serve hot.

Serves 4

Mushroom paprikas

Gombaspaprikas

450g (1lb) mushrooms

3 tablespoons butter

1 medium onion, finely chopped

1 teaspoon paprika, ideally Hungarian

salt

6 tablespoons sour cream or smetana

This dish of mushrooms sauteed in butter with onion, paprika and sour cream is usually served with *galuskas* (dumplings) or rice, but it also makes a very good stuffing for pancakes. As this is such a simple recipe, using the best-quality mushrooms you can find – and, if possible, Hungarian paprika – will make all the difference.

—

Carefully wipe the mushrooms clean, then slice them fairly thinly.

Melt the butter in a heavy frying pan and add the onion. Cook over a moderate heat until it has softened. Add the mushrooms and paprika and mix well. Season with salt, then cook over a moderate heat until the mushrooms are tender and the liquid has reduced. Stir in the sour cream and heat through. Serve at once.

Serves 4

Fennel parmigiana

Finocchi alla parmigiana

4 fennel bulbs

2 tablespoons butter, plus extra for greasing

salt and freshly ground black pepper

100g (1 cup) freshly grated parmesan cheese

For this dish, which is traditionally served for Shavuot, fennel is steamed then lightly fried in butter, topped with grated parmesan and baked in the oven until the top is lightly browned.

—

Trim the ends off the fennel, then cut into wedges. Steam for 10 minutes or until just tender. Melt the butter in a large frying pan and add the fennel. Cook over a gentle heat for 5 minutes, then season with salt and pepper.

Arrange the fennel wedges in a single layer in a well-buttered shallow baking dish and sprinkle over the parmesan cheese. Bake in a preheated 200°C/400°F/gas 6 oven for 15 minutes or until the cheese is golden brown. Serve at once.

Serves 4

Yellow onions with black raisins

Sevoyas amariyas kon pasas

3 tablespoons extra virgin olive oil

½ teaspoon ground turmeric

3 large white or brown onions, thinly sliced

salt and freshly ground black pepper

75g (½ cup) seedless black raisins, soaked for 20 minutes in hot water and drained

This recipe makes a delicious side dish. The onions should be cooked very slowly until they are meltingly soft, but not browned. The raisins add a lovely touch of sweetness.

—

Heat the olive oil in a large frying pan and stir in the turmeric. Add the onions and mix well so they are evenly coated in oil. Season with salt and pepper. Cover and simmer for 30 minutes or until they are very soft, stirring from time to time so they do not stick. Add the raisins and simmer for 5 more minutes. Serve hot.

Serves 4

Baby peas simmered with shallots and white wine

Pisellini cola cegola

3 tablespoons extra virgin olive oil

2–3 shallots, finely chopped

2 lettuce leaves, shredded

450g (2 cups) freshly shelled tender young peas or frozen petit pois

125ml (½ cup) dry white wine

salt and freshly ground black pepper

2 tablespoons finely chopped flat-leaf parsley

This classic Venetian dish is also called *piselli jeuda*, or Jewish peas. Sometimes it is served garnished with lightly toasted pine nuts.

—

Heat the olive oil in a saucepan and add the shallots and lettuce. Cook over a moderate heat until the onion has softened and the lettuce has wilted. Add the peas and wine and bring to the boil. Cover and simmer for 20–25 minutes or until the peas are tender and the wine has almost evaporated. Season with salt and pepper and serve hot, garnished with parsley.

Serves 4

Sweet peppers stuffed with rice, pine nuts and currants

Pimentones reyenades

6–8 medium red or green (bell) peppers

2–3 tablespoons extra virgin olive oil

1 medium onion, finely chopped

180g (1 cup) long-grain rice

handful of finely chopped flat-leaf parsley

2 tablespoons finely chopped dill

3 tablespoons pine nuts

3 tablespoons currants

1 teaspoon sugar

1 medium tomato, peeled, deseeded and chopped

450ml (scant 2 cups) hot water

salt and freshly ground black pepper

Stuffed peppers are often made for Purim and Sukkot, as they are a symbol of abundance. They are also often made for the Sabbath, because they are equally good served hot or at room temperature. In this recipe from Thessaloniki, they are stuffed with a mixture of rice, tomato, pine nuts, raisins and herbs.

—

Brush the peppers lightly with olive oil and place in a well-oiled shallow baking dish. Bake in a preheated 180°C/350°F/gas 4 oven for 10 minutes. Remove the peppers from the oven and, when cool enough to handle, slice off the tops and reserve. Scoop out the pith and seeds from the peppers.

Heat 2 tablespoons olive oil in a heavy saucepan, add the onion and cook over a moderate heat until translucent. Stir in the rice and cook for 2–3 minutes or until it is opaque. Add the herbs, pine nuts, currants, sugar, tomato and 350ml (1½ cups) of the hot water and bring to the boil. Season with salt and pepper, then cover and simmer for 18–20 minutes or until the rice is almost tender.

Stuff the peppers with the rice mixture and place the reserved lids on top. Arrange side by side in a well-oiled shallow baking dish and pour in the remaining hot water. Bake in a preheated 180°C/350°F/gas 4 oven for 40–45 minutes or until the peppers are tender and the stuffing is cooked through. Serve hot or at room temperature.

Serves 4

Hungarian sweet pepper stew

Lecso

900g (2lb) red or green (bell) peppers

4 tablespoons extra virgin olive oil

1 large onion, finely chopped

2 teaspoons Hungarian paprika

675g (1½lb) ripe tomatoes, peeled, deseeded and chopped

salt

One of the classics of Hungarian cuisine, this consists of sweet peppers simmered with onion, tomatoes and paprika. Sometimes one or two hot peppers (called banana chillies or *bogyiszloi*) are included. *Lecso* may be served on its own, with rice or with scrambled eggs. As *lecso* can be served hot or cold, it is often served for the Sabbath.

—

Remove the core, pith and seeds from the peppers and cut into strips about 1cm (½in) thick.

Heat the olive oil in a large frying pan and add the onion. Cook over a moderate heat until it starts to turn golden, then stir in the paprika. Add the peppers, cover and simmer for 10 minutes. Add the tomatoes and season with salt, then cover and simmer for a further 30 minutes or until the peppers are soft. Serve hot.

Serves 4–6

Potato and green olive ragout

Ragout de pommes de terre aux olives

3 tablespoons extra virgin olive oil

1 large onion, finely chopped

900g (2lb) baby new potatoes, cut into halves or quarters

½ teaspoon paprika

dash of cayenne pepper

about 350ml (1½ cups) hot water

100g (1 cup) green olives, pitted and cut in half

freshly ground black pepper

2 tablespoons finely chopped flat-leaf parsley or coriander (cilantro)

In Algeria this is usually made with baby new potatoes. A similar dish is made in Provence with the addition of a few chopped tomatoes – but without the spices.

—

Heat the olive oil in a heavy saucepan and add the onion. Cook over a moderate heat until it has softened. Add the potatoes, paprika and cayenne and stir well. Pour in the hot water and bring to the boil. Cover and simmer for 12 minutes or until the potatoes are almost tender. Add the olives, season with pepper, and continue to cook until the potatoes are tender and the sauce has reduced. Serve hot, garnished with parsley.

Serves 4

Pumpkin, onions and raisins simmered with honey and toasted almonds

Potiron, oignons et raisins secs au miel

1 small pumpkin, about 900g (2lb)

4 tablespoons extra virgin olive oil

900g (2lb) onions, thinly sliced

50g ($\frac{1}{3}$ cup) raisins, soaked in hot water for 30 minutes and drained

1 tablespoon honey or sugar

$\frac{1}{2}$ teaspoon ground cinnamon

$\frac{1}{4}$ teaspoon ground ginger

good pinch of powdered saffron, dissolved in a little hot water

salt and freshly ground black pepper

50g ($\frac{1}{3}$ cup) blanched almonds, lightly toasted in a 180°C/350°F/gas 4 oven until golden

In this dish from the northern Moroccan city of Tetouan, pumpkin is delicately flavoured with cinnamon, ginger and saffron. If pumpkin is unavailable, you can use butternut squash instead. Traditionally, this is served with couscous.

—

Cut the pumpkin in half, peel it and cut into 2cm ($\frac{3}{4}$in) cubes. Steam for 10–15 minutes or until tender.

Meanwhile, heat the olive oil in a large frying pan and add the onions. Cover and cook over a gentle heat for 30 minutes or until very soft. Add the pumpkin, raisins, honey, cinnamon, ginger and saffron and stir well. Season with salt and pepper, then simmer for 5 minutes to blend the flavours. Serve hot, garnished with toasted almonds.

Serves 4–6

Spinach with white beans and tomatoes

Avas kon espinaka

180g (1 cup) dried cannellini or butter (lima) beans

3 tablespoons extra virgin olive oil

1 small onion, finely chopped

3 ripe tomatoes, peeled, deseeded and chopped

450g (1lb) spinach

salt and freshly ground black pepper

Variations of this dish are eaten by Jews across the Balkans – it is often served for Sukkot with a rice pilaf on the side.

—

Soak the beans overnight, then drain.

Place the beans in a saucepan and cover with water. Bring to the boil, then cover and simmer for $1\frac{1}{2}$ hours or until tender. Drain, reserving about 100ml ($\frac{1}{3}$ cup) of the cooking water.

Heat the olive oil in frying pan and add the onion. Cook over a moderate heat until it is softened. Add the tomatoes and continue to cook over a gentle heat for 5–7 minutes or until the sauce is thickened.

Meanwhile, wash the spinach thoroughly and cut into 2cm ($\frac{3}{4}$ inch) strips. Add to the cooked beans, together with the tomato and onion sauce and a few tablespoons of the reserved cooking water. Season with salt and pepper, then simmer for 15 minutes or until the flavours are blended. Serve hot.

Serves 4

Spinach and yoghurt

Bourani-ye esfanaj

450g (1lb) spinach

1–2 tablespoons ghee or butter

1 medium onion, chopped

$\frac{1}{4}$ teaspoon ground turmeric

150g ($\frac{3}{4}$ cup) strained Greek-style yoghurt

salt and freshly ground black pepper

This classic dish can be served as a side dish or appetizer. It is often prepared for Yom Kippur, as well as for the Sabbath.

—

Wash the spinach thoroughly, then cook in a covered saucepan over a moderate heat for 5–7 minutes or until tender – the water clinging to the leaves is sufficient to prevent scorching. Drain well, squeezing out as much moisture as you can. Chop finely.

Melt the butter in a frying pan and cook the onion over a moderate heat until it is tender and starting to turn golden brown. Add the spinach and turmeric and mix well. Simmer for a few minutes to blend the flavours, then remove from the heat. Add the yoghurt and season with salt and pepper. Chill thoroughly before serving.

Serves 3–4

Tomatoes stuffed with rice and mint

Pomodori ripiene di riso

6 large beef (beefsteak) tomatoes

150g (generous ¾ cup) arborio rice

3 garlic cloves, finely chopped

3 tablespoons finely chopped flat-leaf parsley

2 tablespoons finely chopped mint

2 tablespoons torn basil leaves

3 tablespoons extra virgin olive oil

salt and freshly ground black pepper

125ml (½ cup) hot water

This classic dish is often prepared by Roman Jews for the Sabbath. The tomatoes are usually simply stuffed with a mixture of rice and herbs, but the stuffing is also very good with the addition of a little freshly grated parmesan cheese.

—

Slice the tops off the tomatoes and reserve as lids. Scoop out the flesh into a bowl, then add the rice, garlic, parsley, mint, basil and olive oil. Season with salt and pepper and mix well. Spoon the mixture into the tomato shells so they are about three-quarters full, to allow space for the rice to swell during cooking. Place the reserved lids on top.

Arrange the stuffed tomatoes side by side in a well-oiled shallow baking dish and pour in the hot water. Bake in a preheated 190°C/375°F/gas 5 oven for 45–50 minutes or until the rice is tender and the tomatoes are tender but still hold their shape. Serve hot or cold.

Serves 6

Desserts

'Out of snow, you can't make cheesecake'

YIDDISH PROVERB

For most Jews, sweet things are a symbol of happiness and prosperity. Special cakes and pastries are served for every festival, as well as the Sabbath, circumcisions and other special occasions. Jews are renowned for their hospitality, and every Jewish household always has a supply of cakes, pastries or sweetmeats on hand for the unexpected visitor.

Meals usually end with a selection of fresh fruit or fruit compotes, especially in Sephardic households, while Ashkenazi Jews often serve *lokshen* (noodle) or fruit *kugel* (pudding), or strudel – especially for the Sabbath.

Although the Jewish repertoire of cakes and pastries is vast, for this chapter I have chosen a small selection of light cakes and pastries that can easily be made at home, and a variety of fruit desserts, creams and mousses.

Sephardic sponge cake

Pan d'Espanya

4 large eggs, separated

125g (⅔ cup) caster (superfine) sugar

finely grated rind of 1 lemon

100g (¾ cup) self-raising flour

Literally 'bread of Spain', *pan d'Espanya* was probably first introduced to North Africa by Sephardic Jews fleeing the Spanish Inquisition. It is served for most festivals, especially Purim, Yom Kippur and, of course, the Sabbath. Made from eggs, sugar and flour, with no added fat or water, it can be flavoured with vanilla, lemon or orange rind or orange flower water. This light sponge cake is also the foundation of many other desserts, including *paille* – an elaborate cake made for weddings and bar mitzvahs that is soaked in syrup flavoured with rum or orange flower water and layered with fresh fruit or fruit preserves, almond paste and melted chocolate, then topped with meringues.

—

Butter a 20cm (8in) springform cake tin and dust with flour.

Beat the egg yolks and sugar together until pale and creamy, then stir in the lemon rind. In another bowl, whisk the egg whites to stiff peaks, then gently fold into the egg yolk mixture. Gradually fold in the flour to make a smooth batter.

Pour the batter into the prepared tin and bake in a preheated 200°C/400°F/gas 6 oven for 35–40 minutes or until a knife inserted into the centre of the cake comes out clean. Remove from the oven, unclip the tin and allow the cake to cool for 5 minutes. Turn out onto a wire rack and set aside to cool completely.

Serves 6–8

Black cherry cake

Visnova bublanina

450g (1lb) black cherries

75g ($\frac{1}{3}$ cup) butter

100g ($\frac{1}{2}$ cup) caster (superfine) sugar

3 eggs, separated

150g ($1\frac{1}{4}$ cups) plain (all-purpose) flour

finely grated rind of 1 lemon

1 teaspoon baking powder

icing (confectioners') sugar, for dusting

This delicious cake makes a lovely dessert or teatime snack. It is also very good made with plums or apricots instead of cherries.

—

Butter a 20cm (8in) square cake tin and dust with flour.

Wash the cherries and pat them dry. Cut in half and remove the pits.

Beat the butter and sugar together until light and fluffy. Add the egg yolks, one at a time, and mix well. Stir in the flour, lemon rind and baking powder. In another bowl, whisk the egg whites to stiff peaks, then gently fold into the egg yolk mixture.

Pour the batter into the prepared tin and arrange the cherries over the top. Bake in a preheated 190°C/375°F/gas 5 oven for 30–35 minutes or until a knife inserted into the centre of the cake comes out clean. Remove from the oven, unclip the tin and allow the cake to cool for 5 minutes. Turn out onto a wire rack and set aside to cool completely. Dust with icing sugar just before serving.

Serves 6

Almond sponge cake

Boka di dama

6 eggs, separated

150g (¾ cup) caster (superfine) sugar

200g (2 cups) ground almonds

2 tablespoons plain (all-purpose) flour

1 teaspoon baking powder

finely grated rind of 1 orange

1–2 tablespoons orange flower water

This deliciously light almond cake is traditionally served for Purim. The recipe was originally brought to Tunisia by Jews from Livorno, where a similar cake is made. The name *boka di dama* – which literally means 'milady's mouth' – implies that it was delicate enough for a lady's palate.

—

Butter a 23cm (9in) springform cake tin and dust with flour.

Beat the egg yolks and sugar together until light and creamy. Add the ground almonds, flour, baking powder, orange rind and orange flower water and mix well. In another bowl, whisk the egg whites to stiff peaks, then gently fold into the egg yolk mixture.

Pour the batter into the prepared tin and bake in a preheated 180°C/350°F/gas 4 oven for 45–55 minutes or until a knife inserted into the centre of the cake comes out clean. Remove from the oven, unclip the tin and allow to cool for 5 minutes. Turn out onto a wire rack and set aside to cool completely.

Serves 8

Polish honey cake

Honig leiker

175g (1⅓ cups) wholemeal (wholewheat) flour

1 teaspoon baking powder

½ teaspoon bicarbonate of soda (baking soda)

1 teaspoon ground cinnamon

¼ teaspoon mixed spice

¼ teaspoon ground cloves

4 eggs, separated

50g (¼ cup) caster (superfine) sugar

175g (½ cup) honey

3 tablespoons sunflower oil

2 teaspoons instant coffee, dissolved in 75ml (⅓ cup) hot water

40g (⅓ cup) freshly shelled walnuts, coarsely chopped

50g (⅓ cup) sultanas (golden raisins

No Jewish New Year would be complete without a honey cake on the table. *Leiker* (or *lekakh* or *lekeh*) literally means 'a portion' and represents the wish that everyone should have their own abundant portion in the year to come. Honey cake is also served for other festive occasions, especially Purim, weddings and circumcisions. There are many different recipes for honey cake in the Ashkenazi world: some are light and spongy, others are enriched with sour cream. This one from Poland is more dense but has a delicious flavour, and is very good on its own or spread with butter.

—

Grease a 2lb loaf tin and dust with flour.

Sift the flour, baking powder, bicarbonate of soda and spices together into a bowl. Beat the egg yolks with the sugar until light and creamy. Add the honey, oil and coffee and mix well. Add the flour, baking powder, bicarbonate of soda and spices and mix again. Stir in the walnuts and sultanas. In another bowl, whisk the egg whites to stiff peaks, then gently fold into the mixture.

Pour the batter into the prepared tin and bake in a preheated 180°C/350°F/gas 4 oven for 1 hour or until a knife inserted into the centre comes out clean. Remove from the oven, unclip the tin and allow the cake to cool for 5 minutes. Turn out onto a wire rack and set aside to cool completely. Wrap in foil and keep for a day or two before serving.

Serves 8–10

Poppy seed torte

Mohntorte

50g (6 tablespoons) plain (all-purpose) flour

1 teaspoon baking powder

4 tablespoons butter

100g ($\frac{1}{2}$ cup) caster (superfine) sugar

4 large eggs, separated

$\frac{1}{4}$ teaspoon vanilla extract

125g (1 cup) poppy seeds

25g ($\frac{1}{4}$ cup) freshly shelled walnuts, finely ground in a blender or food processor

icing (confectioners') sugar, for dusting

Mohntorte is usually a rich pastry with a poppy seed and raisin filling, but this version from Vienna is a very light cake. Try to find dark blue poppy seeds – they're available in most health food stores and quality delicatessens. *Mohntorte* is usually served for Purim.

—

Butter a 23cm (9in) springform cake tin and dust with flour.

Sift the flour and baking powder together into a bowl. In another bowl, cream the butter with all except 2 tablespoons of the sugar until light and fluffy. Add the egg yolks, one at a time, and mix well. Stir in the vanilla extract, poppy seeds and walnuts and mix well.

In another bowl, whisk the egg whites to soft peaks, then add the remaining sugar and continue whisking to stiff peaks. Gently fold into the poppy seed mixture, alternating with spoonfuls of the flour and baking powder, to make a smooth batter.

Pour the batter into the prepared tin and bake in a preheated 160°C/320°F/gas 3 oven for 40 minutes or until a knife inserted into the centre of the cake comes out clean. Remove from the oven, unclip the tin and allow the cake to cool for 5 minutes. Turn out onto a wire rack and set aside to cool completely. Dust with icing sugar before serving.

Serves 6–8

Chocolate hazelnut cake

Schokolade-haselnusskuchen

butter, for greasing

sugar or potato flour, for dusting

150g (1 cup) hazelnuts

1 teaspoon baking powder

125g (4oz) dark chocolate (70% cocoa solids), broken into squares

5 eggs, separated

1 egg

150g ($\frac{3}{4}$ cup) caster (superfine) sugar

For the icing

125g (4oz) dark chocolate (70% cocoa solids), broken into squares

2 tablespoons rum or hazelnut liqueur

$3\frac{1}{2}$ tablespoons butter

This deliciously flourless chocolate cake is often served during Passover and for special occasions. It is usually topped with a chocolate butter cream icing, but is also very good on its own or topped with whipped cream.

—

Butter a 23cm (9in) springform cake tin and dust with sugar or potato flour.

Place the hazelnuts on a baking sheet in a single layer and roast in a preheated 160°C/320°F/gas 3 oven for 10–12 minutes or until lightly browned, stirring from time so they roast evenly. Remove from the oven and allow to cool slightly. Turn the oven up to 180°C/350°F/gas 4. Process the toasted nuts in a blender or food processor until finely ground. Stir in the baking powder. Melt the chocolate in a heatproof bowl set over a pan of simmering water, taking care not to let the bowl touch the water, then set aside to cool slightly.

Beat the egg yolks and egg with half of the sugar until light and creamy. Add the melted chocolate and mix well, then fold in the ground hazelnuts. In another bowl, whisk the egg whites with the remaining sugar to stiff peaks, them gently fold into the chocolate mixture.

Pour the batter into the prepared tin and bake for 40–45 minutes or until a knife inserted into the centre of the cake comes out clean. Remove from the oven, unclip the tin and allow to cool for 5 minutes. Turn onto a wire rack and let it cool completely.

To make the icing, melt the chocolate in a heatproof bowl set over a pan of simmering water, taking care not to let the bowl touch the water. Stir in the rum, then remove from the heat and beat in the butter, a little at a time, until the icing is smooth and creamy. When the icing is cool but not set, spread over the cake.

Serves 8

Damson tart

Quetschenkuchen

900g (2lb) damsons, cut in half
and stones removed

6 tablespoons sugar, or to taste

1 teaspoon ground cinnamon

icing (confectioners') sugar,
for dusting

For the pastry

100g ($\frac{3}{4}$ cup) plain
(all-purpose) flour

100g ($\frac{3}{4}$ cup) wholemeal
(wholewheat) flour

pinch of salt

100g (scant $\frac{1}{2}$ cup) butter, cubed

2 tablespoons caster (superfine)
sugar

2 egg yolks

5–6 tablespoons iced water
or milk

All kinds of fruit tarts – but especially apricot, cherry, bilberry, plum and damson – are traditionally made by Alsatian Jews for the third meal of the Sabbath. Sometimes a glaze of beaten egg mixed with a few tablespoons of cream or milk is poured over the tart about 10 minutes before the end of cooking. If damsons are unavailable, other purple plums can be used instead. *Quetschenkuchen* is also often served for Yom Kippur.

—

To make the pastry, place the flours and salt on a work surface and make a well in the centre. Using your fingertips, rub in the butter until the mixture resembles coarse breadcrumbs. Add the sugar and egg yolks and sprinkle over the iced water. Working quickly with your hands, form the dough into a soft ball. Wrap in foil and refrigerate for 30 minutes.

Place the dough on a lightly floured board and knead it briefly. Roll out into a circle about 30cm (12in) in diameter and 3mm ($\frac{1}{8}$ in) thick. Carefully roll the dough around the rolling pin and unroll it over a well-buttered 23–25cm (9–10in) tart tin. Ease the pastry into the corners, then trim any excess dough and crimp the edges with a fork. Prick the bottom in a few places. Cover the dough with foil and fill with baking beans to prevent the tart case from puffing up in the oven. Bake in a preheated 200°C/400°F/gas 6 oven for 8–10 minutes. When it's ready, the pastry should have shrunk away slightly from the sides of the tin. Remove from the oven and carefully lift out the foil and beans.

Arrange the damsons in tight concentric circles, cut sides up, over the pastry, then sprinkle with the sugar and cinnamon. Return to the oven and turn down to 190°C/375°F/gas 5. Bake for a further 30 minutes or until the damsons are soft and the pastry is golden. Serve warm, dusted with icing sugar.

Serves 6–8

Pear and walnut strudel

Birnenstrudel

2–3 large sheets of fresh or thawed frozen filo pastry

2 tablespoons melted butter

icing (confectioners') sugar, for dusting

For the filling

3–4 firm but ripe pears

3 tablespoons freshly shelled walnuts, finely ground in a blender or food processor

3 tablespoons sultanas (golden raisins)

3 tablespoons sugar, or to taste

3 tablespoons wheatgerm or breadcrumbs

1 teaspoon ground cinnamon

finely grated rind of 1 lemon

1 tablespoon melted butter

Jewish cooks have been making sweet and savoury strudels ever since the Turks introduced the art of making paper-thin filo or strudel pastry to Europe in the sixteenth century. All kinds of fruit can be made into strudel – especially cherries, apricots and plums – but pears are my favourite. Commercial filo pastry makes it quick and easy to prepare. I often use wheatgerm instead of breadcrumbs, which makes the strudel light and nutritious.

—

To make the filling, peel, core and dice the pears. Place in a bowl and add the walnuts, sultanas, sugar, wheatgerm, cinnamon and lemon rind. Toss lightly, then stir in the melted butter.

Cover the table or work surface with a clean cloth. Lay a sheet of filo pastry on the cloth and brush lightly with melted butter. Repeat with a second sheet of filo pastry. Spoon the filling in a long strip about 7.5cm (3in) wide along the side of the pastry nearest to you and about 1cm ($\frac{1}{2}$in) from the sides.

Carefully lift the corners of the cloth nearest to you so the strudel rolls over on itself. Brush the top lightly with melted butter. Lift the cloth again to allow the strudel to roll over completely. Brush the top lightly with melted butter. Pick up the cloth with the strudel and very carefully twist over onto a greased baking sheet. Brush the top lightly with melted butter. Bake in a preheated 180°C/350°F/gas 4 oven for 30 minutes or until the pastry is crisp and golden. Remove from the oven and cool slightly. Serve hot, warm or cold, dusted with icing sugar.

Serves 6

Peppernuts

Pfeffernuesse

250g (2 cups) wholemeal (whole wheat) flour

½ teaspoon baking powder

¼ teaspoon bicarbonate of soda (baking soda)

½ teaspoon ground cinnamon

½ teaspoon ground cloves

½ teaspoon ground mixed spice

½ teaspoon ground cardamom

½ teaspoon freshly ground black pepper

freshly grated nutmeg

100g (scant ½ cup) butter

75g (⅓ cup) sugar

1 egg yolk

6 tablespoons molasses or black treacle

6 tablespoons brandy

25g (3 tablespoons) raw (un-blanched) almonds, finely ground in a blender or food processor

3 tablespoons finely chopped candied orange peel

finely grated rind of ½ lemon

icing (confectioner's) sugar for dusting

Traditionally served for Purim, these little walnut-sized biscuits are almost cake-like and have a wonderful flavour. If candied orange peel is unavailable you can use mixed peel instead.

—

Sift the flour, baking powder, baking soda and spices together into a bowl.

Beat the butter and sugar together until light and fluffy. Add the egg yolk and mix well, followed by the molasses and brandy. Stir in the almonds, candied orange peel and lemon rind. Gradually add the flour mixture to make a very soft dough.

Shape the dough into small balls about 2cm (¾in) in diameter and flatten slightly. Arrange on a well-greased baking sheet and bake in a preheated 160°C/ 320°F/gas 3 oven for 20 minutes or until they are golden brown. Remove from the oven and allow to cool on wire wracks. Dust with icing sugar.

Makes about 48 biscuits

Sweet pumpkin coils

Rodanchas de kalavassa amarillia

12 sheets fresh or thawed frozen filo pastry, each about 30cm x 18cm (12in x 7in)

extra virgin olive oil, for brushing

icing (confectioners') sugar, for dusting

For the filling

1 small pumpkin, about 900g (2lb)

1 tablespoon extra virgin olive oil

100g ($\frac{1}{2}$ cup) caster (superfine) sugar

1 teaspoon ground cinnamon

2 tablespoons rosewater

100g (1 cup) freshly shelled walnuts, finely ground in a blender or food processor

In the past, these delicious coiled pastries from Thessaloniki were made with homemade pastry, but commercial filo makes them much quicker and easier to prepare. The filling is sweetened pumpkin flavoured with a dash of olive oil, walnuts, cinnamon and rosewater. *Rodanchas* are usually served lightly dusted with icing sugar, and traditionally for Purim.

—

To make the filling, bake the whole pumpkin in a preheated 180°C/350°F/gas 4 oven for 30 minutes or until tender. Remove from the oven and, when cool enough to handle, cut in half and remove the skin, pith and seeds. Place the pumpkin flesh in a large bowl and mash with a potato ricer. Add the olive oil, sugar, cinnamon and rosewater and mix well. Stir in the ground walnuts.

Lay a sheet of filo pastry on a clean cloth, with the longer side facing you, and brush lightly with oil. Spoon a line of filling about 1.5cm ($\frac{1}{2}$in) thick along the long side of the pastry, just inside the edge. Fold the edge over the filling and then roll up into a long, thin log, brushing the filo lightly with oil as you roll. Take hold of one end of the log and loosely roll it up like a coiled snake, being careful not to tear the pastry. Repeat with the remaining pastry and filling.

Arrange the coils side by side on a well-oiled baking sheet and brush the tops lightly with oil. Bake in a preheated 180°C/350°F/gas 4 oven for 15 minutes or until the pastry is crisp and golden. Remove from the oven and set aside to cool. When cold, dust lightly with icing sugar.

Makes 12 pastries

Dried apricot cream

Mishmishiya

300g (2 cups) dried apricots

1 tablespoon rosewater

3 tablespoons sugar, or to taste

200g (1 cup) clotted cream or strained yoghurt

2–3 tablespoons chopped toasted almonds

This simple but elegant dessert is equally good for a dinner party or family meal. There is no need to cook the apricots: you can simply cover them with boiling water and leave them to soak and soften overnight. Once they have been pureed, sweetened and flavoured with rosewater, they are topped with a little clotted cream or strained yoghurt and a scattering of chopped almonds.

—

Place the apricots in a heatproof bowl and cover with boiling water. Cover with a plate and leave to soak overnight.

Drain the apricots, reserving the soaking liquid. Puree the apricots in a blender or food processor with the rosewater, sugar and enough of their soaking liquid to make a thick cream. Chill thoroughly, then pour into individual glass dishes and serve with clotted cream and chopped almonds.

Serves 4

Italian macaroons

Amaretti

100g (1 cup) ground almonds

100g ($\frac{1}{2}$ cup) caster (superfine) sugar

1 large egg white

4–5 drops vanilla extract

16–18 split blanched almonds

These delicious macaroons are crisp on the outside with soft, slightly chewy centres. Their Italian name literally means 'little bitter ones' – most likely because they were originally made with a combination of sweet and bitter almonds, said to enhance their flavour. Italian Jews like to make these for Purim and Passover.

—

Place the ground almonds and sugar in a bowl and mix well. In another bowl, whisk the egg white to stiff peaks, then gently fold in the almonds and sugar, along with the vanilla extract, to form a stiff paste. Shape into small balls about 2.5cm (1in) in diameter. Flatten them into 3cm (1$\frac{1}{4}$in) rounds and top each one with a split blanched almond. Arrange on a baking sheet lined with baking paper leaving enough room for the macaroons to spread slightly. Bake in a preheated 180°C/350°F/gas 4 oven for 12–15 minutes or until pale golden. Remove from the oven and set aside to cool and harden.

Makes 16–18 macaroons

Jahele's apple and pear pudding

Torta Jahele

2-3 tart apples, about 450g (1lb)

2-3 firm but ripe pears, about 450g (1lb)

50g ($\frac{1}{4}$ cup) sugar

1 teaspoon ground cinnamon

50g ($\frac{1}{3}$ cup) raisins

50g ($\frac{1}{3}$ cup) raw (un-blanched) almonds, finely ground in a blender or food processor

50g ($\frac{1}{2}$ cup) breadcrumbs or wheatgerm

3 tablespoons butter

4–5 tablespoons hot water

This simple pudding is perfect for a family dinner. It can be made with apples or pears, or a combination of both. I often use wheatgerm instead of breadcrumbs which makes the pudding lighter and more healthy. In Italy, when the title of a recipe includes the name Jahele or Rachele, Sara or Rebecca, it infers that the dish is of Jewish origin.

—

Peel, core and slice the apples and pears. Arrange a layer of sliced fruit in the bottom of a baking dish. Dust with sugar and cinnamon and scatter over the raisins and almonds. Top with a thin layer of breadcrumbs and dot with butter. Repeat the layers until all the ingredients are used up, ending with breadcrumbs dotted with butter. Carefully pour in the hot water so as not to wash away the breadcrumbs, then bake in a preheated 180°C/350°F/gas 4 oven for 45–55 minutes or until the fruit is tender and the top is golden. Serve hot.

Serves 4

Ashkenazi matzo meal fritters

Bubeleh

4 eggs, separated

4 tablespoons fine matzo meal

olive oil, for frying

icing (confectioners') sugar, for dusting

These deliciously light fritters are traditionally served for Passover. Similar fritters called *friteches* are made by Sephardic Jews from Tunisia, except they are soaked in sugar syrup, rather than being dusted in sugar.

—

Beat the egg whites until they are stiff. In a separate bowl beat the egg yolks lightly and fold into the egg whites. Sprinkle the matzo meal over the top and, using a rubber spatula, lightly fold into the mixture.

Heat a thin layer of oil in a heavy frying pan and drop in heaped tablespoonfuls of the batter. Cook over a moderate heat until the fritters are golden on both sides, then drain on paper towels. Serve hot, dusted with icing sugar.

Serves 4

Cheese blintzes

Kaese Blintzes

2–3 tablespoons butter or oil for frying

icing (confectioners') sugar, for dusting

sour cream, to serve

For the pancakes

125g (1 cup) unbleached plain (all-purpose) flour

pinch of salt

3 eggs

about 350 ml ($1\frac{1}{2}$ cups) milk, or half milk, half water

2 tablespoons melted butter

For the filling

250g (1 cup) curd (farmer's) cheese or ricotta

150g ($\frac{2}{3}$ cup) cream cheese or mascarpone

3 tablespoons sugar, or to taste

2 egg yolks

1 teaspoon vanilla extract

finely grated rind of 1 lemon

These delicious cheese-filled pancakes are much loved by Jews all over central and eastern Europe. The pancakes are usually filled with a mixture of curd cheese and egg yolks or sour cream and a little sugar. Some cooks like to add a few tablespoons of raisins. Traditionally cheese blintzes are served for Chanukah and for Shavuot, which is always celebrated with a dairy meal.

—

Sift the flour and salt into a bowl. Make a well in the centre and drop in the eggs. Gradually whisk in the milk and just enough water (usually about 4–5 tablespoons) to make a smooth batter the consistency of thin cream. Lastly stir in the melted butter. Leave to stand for at least 30 minutes.

Heat a teaspoon or so of butter in a 15-17cm (6-7in) heavy frying pan. When it is hot, pour in $2\frac{1}{2}$-3 tablespoons of batter. Quickly tilt the pan in all directions so the batter evenly covers the base of the pan. The pancake should be very thin. Cook for 1-2 minutes or until the pancake is golden brown on one side. Flip over and cook the other side for about 30 seconds. Set aside and repeat with the remaining batter.

To make the filling, place the curd and cream cheeses, sugar, egg yolks, vanilla extract and lemon rind in a bowl and mix well.

Place a heaped tablespoon of the filling in the lower half of each pancake, browned side facing up. Fold the bottom edge over the filling, then fold over the sides and roll up. Heat a little butter in the same frying pan and fry the blintzes until they are golden on both sides. Dust with icing sugar and serve at once, with sour cream on the side.

Makes 16 pancakes

Apple fritters

Fritelle di mele

4 tart apples

4–5 tablespoons brandy

olive oil, for deep-frying

icing (confectioners') sugar,
for dusting

For the batter

125g (1 cup) unbleached plain
(all-purpose) flour

pinch of salt

1 teaspoon sugar

1 egg, separated

1 tablespoon extra virgin olive oil

3 tablespoons dry white wine

These delicious apple fritters are often made for Chanukah
and Tu Bi-Shevat, the Festival of the Trees. For a variation, try
making them with other fruit, such as bananas, strawberries,
apricots or figs.

—

For the batter, combine the flour, salt and sugar in a bowl and
make a well in the centre. Add the egg yolk, olive oil, wine and
75ml (5 tablespoons) water and mix well, then gradually stir
in up to another 75ml (5 tablespoons) water to make a smooth
batter. Leave to stand for 30 minutes.

Meanwhile, peel and core the apples and cut into rounds about
5mm ($\frac{1}{4}$in) thick. Place in a shallow bowl and pour over the
brandy. Let the apples steep for 30 minutes.

To finish the batter, in another bowl, whisk the egg white until
stiff and then gently fold into the batter. Working in batches,
dip the apple rings into the batter and deep-fry in hot oil until
golden on both sides. Drain on paper towels and serve at once,
dusted with icing sugar.

Serves 4–6

Pomegranate salad

Salade de grenades

4 ripe pomegranates

2 tablespoons sugar, or to taste

1 tablespoon lemon juice

3 tablespoons rum, or to taste

This refreshing fruit salad from Constantine, in the northeast of Algeria, is often served to celebrate the New Year or to break the fast of Yom Kippur. It is generally left all day to macerate, during which time the pomegranates give off a lot of juice.

—

Cut the pomegranates into quarters and scoop out the seeds. Place in a glass serving dish and sprinkle with sugar. Drizzle over the lemon juice and rum, then toss lightly. Cover and leave to macerate in the fridge for at least 4 hours before serving.

Serves 4

Prune and red wine compote

Pfloymen kompot

225g (8oz) prunes

225ml (1 cup) red wine

2 tablespoons sugar or honey, or to taste

½ cinammon stick

2–3 cloves

Dried fruit compotes are traditionally served for the Sabbath by Ashkenazi Jews throughout Eastern Europe. This one is made with prunes, but it could also be made with dried apricots, pears, apples or peaches, and using a split vanilla pod instead of the spices.

—

Place the prunes in a bowl and cover with 225ml water. Leave to soak for at least 2 hours. Transfer to a saucepan and add the wine, sugar and spices. Bring to the boil, then cover and simmer for 20-25 minutes or until the fruit is tender. Remove the spices and chill thoroughly before serving.

Serves 4

Blackcurrant kissel

Kissel

450g (1lb) blackcurrants

3 tablespoons sugar, or to taste

2 tablespoons arrowroot or cornflour (cornstarch), dissolved in 2–3 tablespoons cold water

thick cream or yoghurt, to serve

Kissel is a fruit puree thickened with arrowroot, cornflour (cornstarch) or potato starch: the texture can vary from a fairly thick puree to a thin syrup. Originally it was made with cranberries or loganberries, but today it is made with a variety of fresh or frozen berries. I like to use blackcurrants for their wonderful flavour, but redcurrants, raspberries, strawberries or blueberries can be used instead. It is usually served with cream or yoghurt on the side.

—

Wash the blackcurrants and remove the stalks. Place in a small saucepan with the sugar and 400ml ($1\frac{2}{3}$ cups) water and bring to the boil. Simmer for 5 minutes or until the blackcurrants are soft. Force the blackcurrants through a sieve, then return the puree to the pan and bring to a simmer. Gradually add the arrowroot mixture, stirring constantly, until you have a thick syrup – do not let it boil.

Pour the kissel into individual glass dishes and chill thoroughly. Serve with cream or yoghurt on the side.

Serves 4

Sephardic dark chocolate mousse

Scodelline di cioccolata

100g (3½oz) dark chocolate, preferably 70% cocoa solids, broken into squares

2 tablespoons strong black coffee

3 tablespoons unsalted butter

2–3 tablespoons rum or brandy

3 eggs, separated

2 tablespoons caster (superfine) sugar, or to taste

A *scodelline* is generally a rich almond custard, but this version from Livorno is a rich chocolate mousse delicately flavoured with rum and coffee. It is always best to use organic eggs when they are eaten raw.

—

Melt the chocolate with the coffee and butter over a pan of gently simmering water. Remove from the heat and allow to cool for a few minutes before stirring in the rum. Add the egg yolks, one at a time, using a wooden spoon to mix them in well.

In another bowl, whisk the egg whites to soft peaks, then add the sugar and whisk to stiff peaks. Gently fold into the chocolate mixture.

Spoon the mousse into individual glass dishes and chill thoroughly before serving.

Serves 4–6

Ashkenazi haroset

Charoseth

2–3 small apples, about 250g (9oz), peeled, cored and chopped finely

75g ($\frac{3}{4}$ cup) freshly shelled walnuts, chopped

1 teaspoon ground cinnamon, or to taste

about 120ml ($\frac{1}{2}$ cup) sweet red dessert wine

Charoset or *haroset* is a fruit paste that is traditionally served as part of the Passover ritual table, as a symbol of the mortar used by Jewish slaves in Egypt to build the Pyramids. Recipes vary enormously from country to country. In the Middle East and North Africa it is usually made with a mixture of dried fruit or date syrup, nuts and spices. Polish Jews like to prepare it with chopped apples and walnuts, cinnamon and sweet red wine. The exact proportions and texture can vary from family to family. I like to use different varieties of apples, such as cox, pink lady or jazz. Sometimes raisins are added, or a little sugar or honey. Haroset is usually eaten by the heaped teaspoonful on a small piece of matzo.

—

Place the apples, walnuts and cinnamon in a bowl and mix well. Add enough wine to make a fairly moist paste. Will keep in the refrigerator for up to 2 days.

Makes about 300ml (1¼ cups)

Algerian haroset

Rhailek

225g (1⅓ cups) dates, pitted and chopped

about 175ml (¾ cup) sweet red dessert wine

50g (½ cup) blanched almonds, finely chopped

50g (½ cup) freshly shelled walnuts, finely chopped

¼ teaspoon ground cinnamon

grinding of nutmeg

In this recipe from Algeria, *haroset* – or *rhailek*, as it is usually called – consists of chopped dates simmered in red wine, mixed with chopped nuts and a dash of cinnamon and nutmeg.

—

Place the dates and wine in a saucepan and simmer for 7-8 minutes, stirring constantly, until the mixture has the consistency of jam, adding a little more wine or water if necessary. Remove from the heat and set aside to cool. Add the nuts and spices and mix well. Will keep in the refrigerator for up to 2 days.

Makes about 450ml (2 cups)

Chocolate walnut balls

Karydoglyko

250g (2 cups) freshly shelled walnuts, finely ground in a blender or food processor

4 tablespoons finely grated dark chocolate

3 tablespoons honey, to taste

2–3 tablespoons rum or Marsala

cocoa for rolling (optional)

These delicious little sweets come from the Greek port city of Volos, and they couldn't be easier to make, as they are just ground walnuts mixed with grated chocolate, honey and a little rum or fortified wine such as Mavrodafni or Marsala. Traditionally they are prepared for Passover, weddings and other special occasions, but they are perfect with a cup of Greek coffee at any time of day.

—

Place the walnuts, chocolate and sugar in a bowl and mix well. Add enough brandy to make a smooth, thick paste. Roll into balls about 2cm ($\frac{3}{4}$in) in diameter, then roll in cocoa if desired. Store in an airtight container in a cool dry place for up to 3 weeks.

Makes about 24 balls

INDEX

Publishing Director: Sarah Lavelle
Creative Director: Helen Lewis
Editor: Céline Hughes
Art Direction and Design: Vanessa Masci
Photographer: Mowie Kay
Illustrator: Liz Catchpole
Food Stylist: Maud Eden
Prop Stylist: Lydia McPherson
Production: Tom Moore and Vincent Smith

First published in 2017 by
Quadrille Publishing
Pentagon House.
52–54 Southwark Street
London SE1 1UN
www.quadrille.com

Quadrille is an imprint of Hardie Grant
www.hardiegrant.com

Text © 2017 Paola Gavin
Photography © 2017 Mowie Kay
Illustration © 2017 Liz Catchpole
Design and layout © 2017 Quadrille Publishing

Cataloguing in Publication Data: a catalogue
record for this book is available from the
British Library.

ISBN: 978 1 78713 042 5

Printed in China

ACKNOWLEDGEMENTS

First of all, I would like to thank Diana Henry
for writing so nicely about my three previous
cookbooks on her blog. Without her support
I might never have found my agent, Sonia Land,
who has been so encouraging and supportive
and who helped me find such a good
publishing house.

I would also like to extend a special thanks to
Sarah Lavelle and Céline Hughes, as well as
the designer, Vanessa Masci, at Quadrille, for
producing such a beautiful book. I would also
like to thank my copy-editor, Alison Cowan, for
being so thorough; the food stylist, Maud Eden;
and Mowie Kay for his lovely photographs.

Lastly, I want to thank my three daughters,
Francesca, Bianca and Seana, for all their love
and support while I was researching and
writing this book.